Rebalance Your Voice

By Jaime Vendera

VENDERA PUBLISHING

Vendera Publishing

Interior Design by Daniel Middleton
www.scribefreelance.com

Photography: Sean Daniel
www.SeanDanielmedia.com

Cover Design: Molly Burnside
www.crosssidedesigns.com

Edited by Richard Dalglish

All Italicized wording and Corridor exercise illustrations courtesy of Dr. Ilter Denizoglu and used by permission

"Cleaning and Maintenance" article
Courtesy of Claude LaRoche

ISBN: 978-1-936307-51-7

Printed in the United States of America

NOTE: *Rebalance Your Voice* comes with bonus instructional videos and audio files. To access these files, go to JaimeVendera.com/Members, click on "Rebalance Your Voice." The password is venderavox.

All **bold underline** wording refers to videos and audio files in the Members section

All *italicized sentences and paragraphs* are courtesy of Dr. Ilter Denizoglu and taken from the books, *Textbook of Clinical Vocology* and *Textbook of Pedagogical Vocology*.

The following information is not meant to treat, cure, prevent, or diagnose any vocal-related diseases. Please consult your physician before attempting the following exercises.

CONTENTS

— *Preface from DoctorVOX* —

*J*aime Vendera, a non-aging super-talent and "one who knows too much." From the first moment we met, I felt the turbo engines in his brain, full of new and bright ideas. His intimacy and charity hugs you with a smiling face, and makes you happy to be a friend of him in any condition. His way of understanding things makes you think again in another way. This book will surely help me to think again about what I have created in my DoctorVOX journey.

—DR. ILTER DENIZOGLU

— *My Voice Was Broken . . .*
and I Needed to Fix it. —

Tokyo, Japan, 2014.

Three glasses to shatter in front of several hundred people, and the first one just exploded, with damaging results.

I knew in a split second that I had done serious damage to my voice. I could taste blood running down the back of my throat right after I felt the sting of something piercing the skin behind the opening of my left sinus cavity.

After hundreds of shattered wine glasses, I never thought this would ever happen to me. Yet it did. A small piece of shattered wine glass had shot into my mouth like a tiny bullet. Bullseye, it hit home and would remain in that new home for months to come.

I knew my life had just changed for the worst. Following

is my story of how I am changing it back for the better by learning a new way to "rebalance my voice."

INTRODUCTION

Welcome to *Rebalance Your Voice*. I'm vocal strength trainer and continual book writer, Jaime Vendera. This book, like all my others, started out as a small inkling of an idea and grew into a book. All my books are problem solvers, born out of a question that needed to be answered, usually a vocal problem that a student presented. These include extending range, overcoming hoarseness, and learning how to add a vocal effect like grit to a clean voice without causing damage.

This book is no different, but this time the problem was mine, a one-of-a-kind, freak accident that has caused me, as of this writing, continual vocal pain and daily sporadic bouts of hoarseness for more than four years.

"What? A vocal coach with vocal issues?!?!?"

I assure you, this problem didn't arise from improper vocal technique or vocal abuse. It was the end result of that tiny shard of glass, which led to tissue scarring, nerve damage, and muscular imbalance.

"How could that possibly happen, Jaime? Were you drinking too much wine and decided to eat the glass???"

Hahaha! Not exactly. Well, you already know the answer, but read on for full details.

In the summer of 2014, while performing in Tokyo, on a television show called, "Sekai no hate made Itte Q!" (The Quest), a small shard of glass exploded directly into my mouth, burying itself like a small knife into my throat.

As a professional performer, I knew that the show must go on. I was in mid-performance, with two more glasses to shatter, so I shrugged off the pain and the taste of blood and continued performing. But the horrible, piercing pain persisted. As we finished, the fear of serious damage overwhelmed me.

When I returned to my hotel room, I opened my mouth and looked into the mirror. The back of my throat had a cut and was still bleeding. I felt damaged, physically and mentally, and worried that I had harmed my voice.

I started feeling sick on my flight home. A terrible, two-week cold followed, after which I started to feel somewhat normal again.

After the cold subsided, I noticed that a knot had formed in the back of my throat. Every time I swallowed, the knot felt like a small marble stuck on the left side of my throat. I noticed that even after I got over my cold, I still had daily bouts of hoarseness and momentary voice loss. I paid no attention at first, figuring I just needed time to heal from the accident. But after weeks of pain, with no change, I began to fear the extent of my vocal damage.

Though the fear consumed me, against my better judgement I avoided a visit to the ENT doctor for nearly six months. When I finally went for an examination, it was the usual diagnosis:

"Your vocal cords are fine. Take antibiotics and steroids and you'll return to normal."

Again, against my better judgement, I followed the doctor's orders. As I'd figured, it didn't help; I didn't "return to normal."

I tried other ENTs, to no avail, and my fear continued to grow. Did I have cancer? Had I burst blood vessels deeper inside my tissue that the scope didn't reveal? Had I damaged a vocal muscle? Did I have silent reflux or candida?

I had to know.

After multiples exams, endoscopes, MRIs, and CAT scans, nothing showed; no polyps, no ruptures, no nodules, no glass, nothing. I was told that glass would not show on scans, so I returned my focus to the piece of glass and worried that it was still embedded, causing irreparable damage.

My last ENT told me it was my tonsils. He made sure I knew he was a very smart doctor, much smarter than me, and I was just the patient who, like other patients, got caught up in a Google search of my symptoms. He proceeded to tell me that I had no business, as a non-professional, researching my symptoms because it only led me to believe that a piece of glass caused my problems. His prognosis, he proclaimed, was that it WAS my tonsils. (I had my tonsils removed as a child, but they partially grew back.) Since I had no background to self-diagnose myself, he was right and I was wrong.

He suggested that he remove what was left of my tonsils. (Surgery seems to be the norm among the ENTs I've worked with, save a few who truly care about their patients.)

Got a recurring sore throat, cut those tonsils out; got a nodule, cut it out; got a deviated septum, time for sinus surgery.

While there ARE circumstances when surgery is best, my thinking has always been, "Why aren't doctors focusing on HOW to heal and rehabilitate vocal issues instead of turning to the knife?"

That is one of my pet peeves, and it's why I bypassed my last ENT's "prognosis" and declined to have what was left of my tiny tonsils removed. Many doctors turn to surgery for the quick fix as opposed to addressing WHY the issue occurred in the first place, so that the person can avoid a second surgery if the problem arises again. Many times, it DOES arise again.

That is one of the reasons I wrote this book—to avoid surgery.

You see, not only do I wish to help a student grow as a singer and learn a new way to warm up and train the voice, but I also want to shed some light on an alternative to going under the knife.

Rebalance Your Voice is both a unique approach to warming up and maintaining your voice in order to keep the voice in top shape by building amazingly strong vocal muscles AND a unique method to prevent vocal loss as well as repair vocal damage.

So, what IS the core reason for vocal loss and vocal damage? It is generally a muscular imbalance in the vocal mechanism that has occurred because of a bad vocal habit, such as squeezing the throat and/or using too much breath. Such an imbalance leads to some issue, such as a hoarse voice or, worse, nodules.

The good news is that you're about to learn how to rebalance the voice to eliminate those bad habits and reverse and prevent such issues from arising and recurring.

Let's stop and think for a moment. What if YOU ended up with a vocal issue that caused you to lose your voice for days, weeks, even months on end? What if it even led you to an ENT who said that your only hope was surgery?

That's a scary thought!

Wouldn't you want to know what led you down that path? Even if surgery was the next step, wouldn't you want to find a doctor who could help you find your way back to vocal health after surgery, so that you didn't experience a repeat episode? Wouldn't you want to find an alternative method to reverse the issues without going under the knife?

FYI: I'm not against surgery. I've had neck surgery that

saved me from years of pain. But I prefer the path of preventive maintenance. Sadly, many doctors don't. I hate to be blunt, but many doctors only see "repeat customer" in a patient with nodules and other vocal issues. Remove a nodule today and get paid, and a year down the line, when the nodule returns, remove it again—and get paid again!

This is why I didn't have tonsil surgery. For one, the ENT's diagnosis was 100% incorrect. Even beyond the tonsillectomy, another ENT suggested exploratory surgery to find the center of my issue. One option was burning the ends of the nerves that caused the pain and hoarseness.

Where would this lead? More surgery without my vocal issue being solved, I assure you; only a repeat customer. This is why I searched for another doctor, one who cares about the patient, a doctor who would not view me as a "repeat customer." This is how I found Dr. Ilter Denizoglu.

When searching for doctors who specialize in singers, I discovered a vocal rehabilitation device called the DoctorVOX device, created by Dr. Denizoglu. The DoctorVOX device is a two-part glass mechanism with a round chamber for holding water and a glass tube that splits into two mouthpiece tubes, one for vocalizing into the water to create a "vocal massage" effect, the other for inhaling moistened air.

I reached out to DoctorVOX and befriended Dr. Denizoglu's business partner, Atilla Ozbilen. Atilla sent me a DoctorVOX device, and after reading the instructions and performing the exercises, I noticed some relief from the pain caused by the knot in my throat. But since the DoctorVOX device was made of glass, I worried that I'd accidentally break it when I was flying around the world for various television shows and workshops.

I wished there were a more compact, non-breakable version. That's when it dawned on me—what if the tube part of the DoctorVOX device were made of plastic or rubber so that it could be attached to any water bottle? What if it were small enough to pack for traveling to gigs? What if you could fit it in your back pocket?

That's when I contacted Mr. Ozbilen and Dr. Denizoglu and urged them to create a new device that you could carry in your pocket and use with any water bottle. Thus, by my encouragement, the pocketVOX was born. In fact, it was shocking how quickly they released this new product. It was a matter of only a few months!

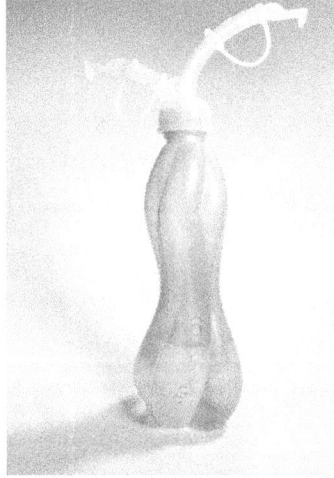

I finally met Dr. Denizoglu in 2016 while I was conducting an "Extreme Vocals" workshop as a guest of famed Polish vocal coach Sonia Lachowolska in Krakow, Poland. He examined me and determined that I indeed had been cut by glass and might have had some stuck in my throat for several months. He reassured me that the glass was either already dissolved by my body or pushed out through the pharyngeal wall.

He then performed on me what he referred to as "shiatsu of the voice."

Dr. Denizoglu says,

> *Shiatsu is another name for acupressure, which is an ancient Chinese traditional application that refers to applying manual pressure on acupuncture points.*

By the time he was finished with my first therapy session, I could barely speak. The exam and treatment proved that I had some sort of vocal issue that was irritating my nerves and possibly causing a muscular imbalance.

I assumed the worst—that I would need surgery. But, although he's a successful phono-surgeon who has treated more than 100,000 voice patients, Dr. Denizoglu believed that my voice could heal WITHOUT surgery!

In an attempt to self-heal, I spent the following 18 months working with the pocketVOX by my side. Finally, in the summer of 2018, I met again with Atilla Ozbilen and Dr. Ilter Denizoglu when they invited me to stay with them in Phila-delphia, where Dr. Denizoglu was presenting at the 2018 Care of the Professional Voice con-ference.

While in Philadelphia, he re-examined me twice, performed more "shiatsu of the voice," and reassessed my vocal issue. He discovered that the physical adjustments I'd made to deal with the knot and the pain had weakened and created imbalance within the three major sets of vocal muscles, the posterior cricoarytenoid, the thyroarytenoid, and the cricothyroid muscles.

This turned his role from doctor to vocal coach. He took me through a voice lesson to learn a new approach to performing exercises, one that's very similar to my Isolation exercises, as explained in my book *Raise Your Voice*. The new approach was intended to help me find balance again between my muscle groups.

To help YOU rebalance YOUR voice, you must first understand what I went through, which is why I want to begin this book by sharing with you one of my vocal lessons with Dr. Denizoglu. It's not pretty, but by hearing me at my worst, you'll have a better understanding as we proceed.

Dr. Denizoglu Voice Lesson

I won't lie—the routine was and still is extremely challenging for me. While the voice lesson in and of itself focused mainly on an exercise he created called the Corridor exercise (a modified version of my Siren exercise), other unrecorded lessons showed me new ways to perform my Transcending Tone and E-Scream exercises (from *Raise Your Voice)* to create the perfect routine for my daily vocal rehabilitation sessions.

At the time of this writing, I have not fully recovered from of the damage caused by that little piece of glass, and because of the scarring I may never fully recover. BUT, I have found new ways to help rebalance my voice so that I have been able to continue teaching, singing, even shattering wine glasses.

I've shared my rebalancing routine with my students, even showed them ways of performing my Isolation exercises with DoctorVOX tools. By incorporating these rebalancing techniques, I've not only helped my students warm up quicker and build a better voice faster, but I've also seen vast improvement in those who had vocal issues before coming to me. Now my wish is to share my findings and my journey with you!

By modifying my approach from "strength training" to include "vocal rebalancing," I have gotten much closer to 100% and discovered new ways to help singers facing vocal hurdles reach their maximum potential.

Your journey to your own maximum vocal potential begins by learning the basics of rebalancing in Chapter One.

CHAPTER ONE

— *Rebalancing Basics* —

Before we dive into the tools and exercises for rebalancing your voice, we'll start with a basic background on the hows and whys of the methodology we will be using.

The tools involved in rebalancing your voice can be found at DoctorVOX.US. While we will cover the DoctorVOX device, we will primarily be using a pocketVOX, bottleVOX, maskVOX, and (optional) Lax Vox tube. Why are these tools so powerful?

Because they are based on the principles of DVT therapy and SOVT (Semi-Occluded Vocal Tract) exercises, reformulated to form DoctorVOX Therapy (DVT therapy).

DVT therapy can alleviate vocal fatigue and even reverse vocal issues such as mutated falsetto, bowed cords, and nodules.

While this book does not explain DVT therapy, because the tools and exercises used in DVT therapy will vary from patient to patient, I will share the DVT therapy program prescribed by Dr. Denizoglu for my unique case.

If you'd like to learn more about DVT therapy, please refer to the following books, written by Dr. Denizoglu:

> *Textbook of Clinical Vocology*
> *Textbook of Pedagogical Vocology*

Regardless, using these tools to vocalize through a tube into water can produce amazing results. Let's start at the beginning by learning the history behind DoctorVOX. The following is taken directly from Dr. Denizoglu to explain the origins of DoctorVOX tools and DVT therapy:

Marketta Sihvo, Ph.D., a Finnish speech and voice therapist, introduced her Lax Vox method, giving workshops at numerous international voice conferences since early 1991. She got the idea to give her patients a "tube and bottle" of water for phonating into water through a flexible silicon tube. Most of them were surprised, curious, and liked it. In a few minutes, the user can perceive the idea of healthy voice production. Sihvo's silicone Lax Vox tube is an easy tool to carry in the pocket or handbag and to be used to warm up and cool down the voice system before and after a demanding vocal task, or when necessary and for fun.

By adequate questions the 'laxvoxer' may be led to insights, to consciousness and knowledge of the possibilities of own voice control and, obviously, of his or her (bad) vocal habits. Own insights are assuring and easy to believe, and clearer than any verbal explanations. This method teaches a way to help oneself, to prevent vocal failures and to find relief.

A Turkish laryngologist, Ilter Denizoglu, attended to Sihvo's workshop at PEVOC 2003 in Graz. Later, he used his professional knowledge to explain why the phonation into water through a tube is experienced so effective. He created a crucial supplement to Sihvo's workshop with his excellent explanations on the interactions between anatomical physiological, physical, and acoustical aspects. To

Rebalance Your Voice

put it short, the oral pressure, increased by water, widens the vocal tract during phonation, provides safe and economic vibration for the vocal folds, and preventing harmful tensions in the laryngeal area. The tube between protruded lips serves as a voice tract extension that has an impact on the sound. The biofeedback helps the laxvoxer to become conscious of his or her way of healthy voice production. Phonation into a tube with one end in water is a simple way to immediately correct and facilitate the function of the vocal mechanism in short time.

From the time that Dr. Denizoglu was introduced Sihvo's Lax Vox technique, he created a full system combining medical, pedagogical, and physical principles, which he named DoctorVOX Therapy (DVT). DVT is a combination of patient evaluation, followed by an individually designed voice therapy program with DoctorVOX devices and various exercises to meet the patient's needs. DVT exercises and devices change the user's behavior and attitude, bringing freedom and joy to voice use. Thus being a holistic method that affects the interaction of phonation, posture, breathing, laryngeal at all pitches. This is a cognitive approach giving multichannel biofeedback. DVT can be applied to vocal pedagogy for being a useful tool for starting voice cure, care, and vocal education and adopting good vocal habits. Singers may apply DVT exercises into their normal daily practice and singing tasks.

The vocal exercises in this book, when combined with any DoctorVOX device, create a "back pressure" effect, which leads to a reverse air pressure returning to the vocal cords. This type of exercise is known as an SOVT exercise. As previously mentioned, SOVT stands for "semi-occluded vocal tract."

A semi-occluded vocal tract occurs when the sound of your voice is partially restricted from leaving your mouth, creating a "back pressure" or a "pressure of your sound" reflecting back down the pharynx (vocal tract), where it returns to your vocal cords. This gentle "sound reinforcement" placed upon the cords results in more ease of vocal cord vibration with less muscular effort.

SOVT exercises can be done with a straw alone, a straw in water, or by exercises such as humming or lip bubbles. The positive effects are many, including less impact, collision, and stress on the vocal cords as they continue to stretch in a balanced position.

The balance of air pressure in the vocal tract is a huge contributor to vocal cord vibration. Without the air pressure in the vocal tract, the vocal cords cannot vibrate, because it is a system of balance above and below the vocal cords.

If this is confusing, think of it like this: the air from the lungs is converted into sound as it passes between your vibrating vocal cords, which are trying to resist the release of air. This converted sound then travels up the pharynx (or vocal tract), leaving the mouth. When the pathway out of the mouth is partially blocked (semi-occluded), the sound pressure that does not fully escape the mouth is converted into "back pressure," which will travel back down the pharynx to the initial vibrating source (vocal cords).

When this back pressure affects the vibrating waves of the vocal cords, the result is a wider, more relaxed vocal tract. It also improves the efficiency of vocal cord vibration in conjunction with reducing the amount of muscular stress involved in vocal sound production.

I've used SOVT exercises for years. Lip bubbles were the first warmup exercise I ever learned from my vocal coach, Jim Gillette.

Even before Jim, I played with SOVT exercises and didn't even know it. I loved to hum into kazoos to feel the vibrations in my throat. I also liked to hum into harmonicas and pitch wheels to match the notes with my voice instead of blowing on the holes.

Yes, I was a strange musical kid. I loved sound and the sensation of sound. One time when I was cleaning my aquarium, cleansing the large tubing used for air release, I put it to my lips and blew bubbles into a sink full of water. I know, gross, hahaha. Don't ask me why; remember, I was a weird kid. :)

Next, I hummed into the tube. I could feel a massive wall of sound vibrating down into my throat as if the aquarium tubing had started vibrating and grew down inside my throat until it reached my vocal cords.

The sensation reminded me of the vibrations I felt when I placed my hand on the speaker cone of my keyboard amp and hit some keys on my synth. The speaker would vibrate wildly and tingle my fingers. When I hummed through the tube it felt like my voice was tingling too, almost as if my vocal cords were being massaged by the sound waves.

The vibration from humming through tubing into water was far superior to the kazoo. I became so obsessed with this feeling that I began humming through my straw any time I was drinking soda from a fast food restaurant.

For me, the feeling of vocalizing through a tube into water was the most efficient way of creating back pressure. But why? Why did it feel better than humming into a harmonica or performing lip bubbles?

Because humming through a tube into water creates both

AC and DC current. This analogy was coined by Dr. Denizoglu. He states,

> Types of back pressure during SOVT exercises may be classified according to the temporal and spatial characteristics of physical effects. SOVT exercises can be classified according to the duration and amplitude of impact of the back pressure. If there is a constant back pressure, we can call it DC-SOVT, and it can be applied in two levels of back pressure.
>
> Narrow drinking straws, a hand placed over the mouth exercise, and voiced fricative consonants such as sustaining a "Z" consonant provide a high constant (DC) back pressure, whereas nasal consonants (humming) and semivowels such as "Y" or "W" provide a low DC back pressure on the system.
>
> If the back pressure impact is very fast and short, we can speak about transitory back pressure with voiced stop consonants such as [b], [g], [d].
>
> In alternating back pressure (AC) current, the accessory system works in an oscillatory fashion as in so-called trills (lip bubbles, tongue trills, etc.).
>
> The last SOVT type is known as blowing into tubes in water. DVT devices provide both AC and DC back pressure in an adjustable fashion together at the same time. The new DoctorVOX-elite has a cylindrical built-in valve in order to fine-tune the DC back pressure.

Think of it this way. Vocalizing through a straw without water (with the exception of lip bubbles and tongue trills) will create DC current, or vocal current that steadily flows one way—out of the mouth through a "compressed" area. We do still have back pressure with these exercises, like the one-way flow of current from a DC battery. But, when we vocalize through a tube into water, it creates more of the pressure that flows both ways simultaneously for more equal balance, with continually changing pressure due to how fast the water bubbles, thus creating both AC and DC current. The water absorbs the release of sound, which then resonates back up the tube and down the throat to its source of origin, the vocal cords, making vocal cord vibration much more efficient.

HOW does this actually "help" voice production?

Glad you asked. Since we're getting a little "science-y," it's time for a basic science lesson.

Those who know me know that I generally avoid the "science approach" to teaching voice, because I prefer to leave that to the ENTs and vocal scientists. But, for the sake of this book, it's important to briefly expand into the area of science for those who want a better understanding. Here we go:

The air that travels between the cords creates a positive vibration, which turns into sound that is bouncing around in the vocal tract above the vocal cords, building resonance and taking tonal shape via the articulators (teeth, tongue, etc.) before that sound leaves the mouth.

Remember, sound is created when the vocal cords vibrate. They vibrate because of air release from the lungs trying to find "balance" between the negative pressure we get from above the cords and the positive air pressure below the cords. As this air passes between the cords, we get the Bernoulli Effect via the vocal cords. Blow between two sheets of paper stacked together and you will notice how they "pull" back together as you blow them apart.

This continual tradeoff between the positive air pressure

below the cords, which needs to "fill up" the negative air space above the cords, will cause the cords to suck together from above and burst apart from below, thus creating sound.

When vocalizing through a tube in water, you'll get more "push" from above, resulting in less push from below. In simpler terms, using the tube minimizes the negative air space above the cords, which means less space that needs to be filled up from the positive air pressure below the cords. This results in less muscular involvement to create pitch, which equals less vocal fold fatigue.

I liken this to two of the same ends of a magnet (positive to positive) pressing against each other. Dr. Denizoglu refers to the softer analogy of *each end of a hand scale balancing each side.*

By performing vocal exercises with a tube in water, you will balance the air pressure above and below, which will "massage the cords." This will warm up the vocal cords more quickly and efficiently. It will also help correct vocal issues (such as imbalanced cords, nodules, etc.) and strengthen the overall mechanism, improving coordination, range, stamina, and tone, while also smoothing out vocal breaks.

The positive results of vocalizing through a tube into water are noticed within minutes when performed correctly. As for how long the effect lasts, it is different for everyone. I liken it to wearing roller skates. As a kid, when I was skating, I felt as if I was in constant, effortless movement. When it was time to take off my skates and return them to the rental counter, I still felt as if I was wearing them. For a few minutes afterward, I seemed to effortlessly stride across the floor, as if I were still wearing roller skates.

Dr. Denizoglu likens this effect to an orthopedic shoe, because the effects of the straw help reduce the stress impact on the vocal cords. He says,

Using the DVT devices resembles orthopedic shoe treatment in physical therapy / orthopedics. A patient with a gait disorder, let's say, steps with their right foot rotated 30 degrees inward. The orthopedic shoe will prevent this kind of stepping and create a new balance among the muscles and joints. If the patient walks with this specific orthopedic shoe, in several weeks (generally motor learning takes approximately six weeks) if not months, he / she will be able to step (without the orthopedic shoe) as the orthopedic shoe forced the right foot to step correctly.

That's why I have named it the "orthopedic shoe effect" for the outcome of the use of the DVT devices. During phonation into the DVT devices, the voice system takes a "factory setting" position; a comfortable low laryngeal posture, with a safe and effective vocal fold vibration pattern, and correct abdominodiaphragmatic breathing, etc.

When the patient properly uses the device with proper exercises customized by the clinician, the dysphonia will be replaced by proper phonation technique.

Using DoctorVOX tools, such as a pocketVOX to warm up the voice and a maskVOX to sing, will help your mind-body coordination improve because of the "factory setting" of the voice. If you vocalize within moments after using these tools, you will retain some of that muscle memory for a short time. Eventually, the results become permanent because continual use results in muscle memory retention.

So, what makes a pocketVOX any better than a tube?

For one, Dr. Denizoglu designed the pocketVOX and DoctorVOX device to mimic the length of the vocal tract.

This can affect the acoustical properties of the vocal tract and minimize involvement of the medial muscles involved in vocalizing, an additional benefit. Remember, less involvement equals less stress.

Second, the tubes used in the DoctorVOX tools are arched so that the user does not have to bend the head and distort the neck and path of the vocal tract.

Third, each tool has measure marks to adjust the volume of water. Each pocketVOX has marks that allow the user to change the length of the tube by cutting the tip, which provides a better approximation of vocal tract length per vocal categorization (bass, baritone, tenor, alto, soprano) in a man, woman, or child. Each DoctorVOX device has a rubber extension tip for lengthening the glass tube to approximate vocal tract length.

Last, a second, smaller tube allows the user to inhale the evaporated water within the bottle to help moisten the cords.

After using one of the tools, whether it's a rubber tube or a DoctorVOX product, you will feel more ring in your tone (or more buzz in the voice). At this point, feel free to try it. Grab a tube and stick it into a bottle of water. Better yet, if you have your pocketVOX, vocalize into the longer tube and you'll notice the strong vibration created around your vocal cords.

When using water, you not only can feel the vibration but also see the results of your work. By producing steady bubbles into water, you're producing steady airflow and creating adequate back pressure.

Hopefully, you now have a basic understanding of this amazing process. For a more advanced discussion on how vocal anatomy and DVT therapy affects the voice, I HIGHLY suggest that you go to DoctorVOX.com to purchase Dr. Denizoglu's books, the *Textbook of Clinical*

Vocology and the *Textbook of Pedagogical Vocology*, which delve much deeper into this subject.

Before moving on, I want to touch on why I've continued to say "tube" and not "straw." I've always preferred using tubes, as I am not as big a fan of straws, including regular drinking straws and coffee straws, as I am of larger tubing. Why?

For one, I've never physically felt the same benefit from vocalizing through a straw as I have when vocalizing through a larger tube or a pocketVOX with a bottleVOX. Yes, I've tried larger-diameter straws in water, and they do work well, but not as efficiently as a pocketVOX.

I don't feel that regular plastic straws do much for my voice, and smaller coffee straws are a no-go for me. Many reading this statement will beg to differ, but I stand my ground. I feel that vocalizing though such a small-diameter straw causes too much back pressure and leads to imbalance. Hey, I've tried them. I've used stirring straws, coffee straws, small aluminum snuff sniffers, and even tiny metal straws peddled for singers. All of these small straws made my voice feel tight and uncomfortable.

I've known amazing coaches who swear by the coffee straw. Great for them, I'm glad they helped; but my students who have tried small straws have initially reported similar findings as I've experienced.

I attribute this to a muscular issue. If your vocal muscles are well-developed, the coffee straw can work once you put in the practice time required to find the balance for vocalizing through such a tiny space; I am not refuting it. In fact, for the sake of study, I've continued to work with a coffee straw for some time, and eventually most of the discomfort I initially experienced disappeared as I found a way to readjust my air-flow balance. But I do notice that my high range is slightly hampered when vocalizing through a coffee straw, and I still feel less vibration and some minute constriction.

Bottom line, I've never felt as vocally free when using a tiny straw as I do when using a pocketVOX. Nor did I feel the tremendous amount of vibration that I do with DoctorVOX devices.

I must add that while I am not a fan of coffee straws, I have found benefit from performing an exercise that constricts breath release in a similar way. This is an exercise called Microbubbles that I teach in my *Four-Week Vocal Break Eraser* program (available at SingBetterFast.com). Microbubbles are similar to lip bubbles, but the lips are pressed flat as you vocalize on a sustained "vvvvvvvvvvvvvv."

Microbubbles seem to produce a similar "coffee straw" effect, but I find better balance with the vvvvvvvvvvvvvvs than I do when vocalizing through a coffee straw, because I can control the amount of air release by adjusting my lips to allow more or less.

Not to worry, we won't be using straws for this process. This book is a how-to manual for DoctorVOX users to get the best they can out of these devices when combined with the methods and exercises I teach in *Raise Your Voice* and at VenderaVocalAcademy.com.

Now back to DoctorVOX devices. In my opinion, these are the best tools to use for SOVT exercises. In fact, think of *Rebalance Your Voice* as the basic how-to manual that comes with your new DoctorVOX tools, whereas Dr. Denizoglu's books are what you'd study for advanced application and understanding.

Before diving deeper into this methodology, our next chapter covers some basic terms that you'll see throughout this book.

CHAPTER TWO
— *Rebalancing Terminology* —

The following terms are key to learning the techniques in this book. Dr. Denizoglu will present the definitions, and I will sum up each term. Please study and commit to memory these terms before moving on:

Primal Sound – The *primal sound is a reflexive, safe, and economical way of vocalizing. It has been introduced by Oren Brown as it applies to singing pedagogy and voice therapy. Primal sounds are those sounds that humans tend to make instinctively as emotional responses. When discussing primal sounds, Oren Brown says, "We humans, like all animals, create sound to express our various states and needs. These sounds are involuntary; they spring from our emotions."*

Brown goes on to say, "Primal sound...is the sound you make without thinking when, for example, you are amused, or startled, or enraged."

Janice Chapman, in her nucleus satellite model, mentioned the core components, which are the primal sound, postural alignment, breathing, and support. Then come the others: speaking voice, resonance, articulation, artistry, and performance for vocal training. Primal sound is the first and the most important step of singing pedagogy. During phonating with primal sound, the muscles of the vocal system are held in their optimal tonus, or optimal tonal position, so every movement may be executed freely and safely. The implications include: the largest pitch range, safe loudness levels, and the most economical use of vocal apparatus.

For me, the meaning of the primal sound is the childhood voice, which doesn't contain any lies, any vanity, or artificiality. The primal sound may not be felt as if it is under control, but it doesn't need control. It is involuntary because you don't need to think and design the sound; it just comes out. Primal sound is not much, but not less either. With the primal sound, "enough is enough" or a more fashionable term, "less is more."

Primal sound is the instinctive balance between breath management, adjustment of the articulators, and laryngeal action. This is why the primal sound is so important and concerned as a crucial step in DVT.

To sum up Dr. Denizoglu's wording, the primal sound is your raw, true, uninhibited vocal sound. It is your instinctive tone that is produced when the cords come fully together for maximum vibration and balance. One of my beloved vocal coaches, Elizabeth Sabine, based her entire teaching methodology on the emotional release of primal sounds, such as the baby cry.

Primal Sound

False Vocal Folds (FVF) – *The false vocal folds (FVF) are a pair of valves placed just above the "true" vocal folds (vocal cords); but we don't want* *them to interfere with phonation, especially in singers, and especially in high notes. Though, sometimes we like to hear their sound (heavy metal, tuvan throat singing, etc).*

You can think of the FVFs as the "valve-like organs" of creating what I call the "trying hard reflex." This reflex appears when we especially need to increase the intrathoracic pressure. It is helpful, not a sin. Many movements such as coughing, carrying heavy luggage, defecation, or bearing a baby are made by the help of FVFs. This is a rule of physiology.

Another important move which activates the trying hard reflex happens during singing. Singers tend to contract the FVFs when they sing high pitches and at high loudness levels, which is when vocal strain occurs. We do not want this to happen. So, the Corridor exercise in DVT provides to control the contraction of the FVFs so they do not come into play during singing.

So you see, the FVFs do NOT need to come into play during high notes. Moreover, they are not "falsetto cords," therefore not responsible for creating falsetto. They can, however, manipulate sound in such a way as to create aggressive tones, like grit or Tuvan throat singing tones.

The Muttley Laugh – *The Muttley laugh (named so after the laugh of a beloved cartoon character) or silent laugh maneuver helps to feel and monitor the FVF contraction. During this maneuver, the FVFs open (as in pre-yawn position); on the other hand during whispering in high loudness, they close. By* *this way, the singer can understand how to prevent reflexive supraglottic squeeze and control the FVF contraction on will. Especially during high pitches, this helps to decrease the hyperfunction and uncontrolled voicing.*

The Corridor exercise of DVT combines the correct downward-forward tilt of the thyroid cartilage (by CT muscle activity) with keeping the supraglottic space open by the focused effort on FVFs. Since the reflexive closure of FVFs are possible not only with trying hard but also singing high and/or loud pitches and also in heavy whispering, we must learn how this feels so that we can avoid this trying hard contraction of the FVFs on high notes.

The Muttley laugh is supposed to promote active (and conscious) FVF opening. It may take time to acquire this skill for a delicate control. The fish smile may also help to support the vocal tract to some extent, with a pre-yawn position, supporting the raising of the soft palate and opening of FVFs as well. By doing the Muttley maneuver, it gives you the one extreme of FVF OPENİNG contraction especially on high notes.

For the life of me, I could not understand this concept, and had bugged Dr. Denizoglu repeatedly to understand *why* he was using this sound to open the vocal cords. I was wheezing to get this sound out, and I could feel clamping in my throat. For me, this was NOT an open feeling—until he simplified it even further:

This maneuver is a bit tricky. If it sounds as if you're wheezing from the bronchi (the lungs), then you are performing this maneuver correctly. If it sounds and feels as if the wheezing *comes from your larynx, then you're squeezing your throat; this is not the Muttley.*

It is an openness in the throat, not like whispering. It does need effort to keep the FVFs open; but this effort easily comes from the essence of the pre-yawn (not a full yawn) position.

Once I got the wheezing out of my throat and only heard and felt it in my lungs, I understood. By practicing the Muttley sound, you will get an extreme version of openness that is a wider sensation in the throat than even a pre-yawn (micro-breath on a yawn for all you *Raise Your Voice* aficionados) position. Thus, you will be able to *feel* when the FVFs contract (like on a loud whisper or when grunting) and correct the issue.

Remember, you should always aim for a relaxed opening in the pharynx. This is why I've adopted the "micro-breath on a yawn" approach on every inhale before I sing. This is a quick, surprised type breath that raises the soft palate, drops the jaw, lowers the larynx, and helps the FVFs remain open, all in order to prevent unnecessary "squeeze" in the throat. The micro-breath is also the same as Dr. Denizoglu's fish smile.

Muttley Laugh

Low Falsetto – *Low falsetto = low larynx. This tone is used in yodeling, and is more of a hollowed, or hooty owl sound.*

If you yawn as you sustain a falsetto tone, you'll hear a

dark, hollow sound, which is your low falsetto.

> **High Falsetto** – *High falsetto = high larynx. This tone is more of a high, thin "eeeee" type falsetto sound, which may be breathy.*

While it may be breathy, as Dr. Denizoglu states, it can be cleaned up, but a breathy tone is generally related to high falsetto. This is the Mickey Mouse voice and the same sound I make when I shatter wine glasses with my voice, although the actual tone I use is more of what I call a pharyngeal tone or reinforced falsetto, or as Dr. Denizoglu explains in the next definition, a "supported falsetto."

> **Supported Falsetto** – *Loud, bright falsetto, the sound that countertenors make in opera, known as chiaroscuro.*

Again, I call this type of falsetto a "reinforced falsetto" or "pharyngeal voice." It's a bright, piercing, and somewhat abrasive falsetto-type tone. It's the same tone I use to shatter glass. For those of you who studied *Raise Your Voice*, you understand that this is not entirely falsetto but a blend of falsetto and full voice. On my 1-10 scale in *Raise Your Voice*, this tone, albeit very loud, is around 3-4.

Before moving on, I'd like to say that I personally love using falsetto in certain songs. I love the tonal variations I can create from breathy to pure to bright to dark. It is a great tool for coloring your songs. There is however a condition called mutated falsetto. Mutated falsetto (better known as Puberphonia) is a voice disorder that refers to the habitual use of a high-pitched voice when speaking.

I first noticed this condition years ago from a contestant

on American Idol. He sang in falsetto and then he spoke in a Mickey Mouse tone. I originally thought he was intentionally speaking in falsetto to stand out among the other contestants, and only learned years later that this voice disorder existed.

While some who experience mutated falsetto may have the Mickey Mouse tone, it may also be heard as breathy, rough, even lacking power. I only bring this up now to assure you that falsetto IS a valid tone for singing, BUT, if you feel "stuck" in falsetto when you speak and sing, there has been studies conducted using DVT therapy, which have proven successful in correcting this voice disorder.

Falsetto Variations

Posterior Cricoarytenoid (PCA) Muscles – *Of the three muscle groups, the PCA helps to keep the low voice alive below the first break. Many singers have breathy voices on low notes, which is a sign of weak PCAs. Some teachers tend to say, "Sing as if you're breathing in" to help clean up breathy, low notes. This is really a myth, as we phonate only when we breathe out. However, some creepy sounds can be produced with a reverse vibration of the vocal folds (while inhaling) but we do not use it during singing. The PCA muscle is also the major muscle for opening the vocal folds, WITH the diaphragmatic contraction simultaneously.*

So if you can manage keeping your PCA (diaphragm as well) relaxed through contraction, it will give you an active counter-balance for the vocal folds. Especially on low tones, the vocal folds tend to be sluggish and the larynx is pushed down with a discomforting breathy unnatural sound. Controlling the PCA helps to keep the glottic posture "alive" during gliding, especially on the lower tones. Otherwise, the pushed larynx would be used to create a low note, which can lead to vocal stress.

I have seen the pushed (or forcibly lowered) larynx occur with many students trying to clean up their lower notes and/or add lower range. When we strengthen the PCA, we do not need to push the larynx down for a solid low voice.

Thyroarytenoid (TA) Muscles – *Of the three, the TA is in dominance for the low and mid-range of the voice (chest register), and it takes over dominance with its changing parts (medial and lateral).*

This muscle is heavily involved in closing the throat when swallowing, as well as cord closure, and the dominant muscle we use in our speaking voice

Cricothyroid (CT) Muscles – *Of the three, the CT takes over dominance in the high voice above the second break (roughly C5-D5 in males, E5-G5 for females). However, the naive contraction of CT leads to phonation in the falsetto register. The singer must coordinate and balance the two pitch mechanisms (TA and CT) all the time, otherwise the voice will flip into falsetto. This, of course, is in combination with all of the other intrinsic and even extrinsic muscles of the larynx.*

Dominance of this muscle is what lends to the "thinning of the voice" on higher notes and maintaining more "full voiced" and "blended" tones as opposed to flipping into falsetto.

In actuality, ALL THREE sets of muscles MUST ALWAYS be in a state of contraction when singing. However, one set of the three muscles should be in dominance based upon "where" you are singing in your range.

Now that you've been schooled, haha, it's time to meet the rebalancing tools. Let's move on.

CHAPTER THREE

— *Rebalancing Tools* —

The following section contains all of the DoctorVOX basic devices that I am currently using. The videos provided with this book will give you a better understanding of each device and how to use them. Please refer to the Members section of this book many times. As new devices are developed, I will add new videos, even if the device is not covered in this book. Following is a review of each tool taken directly from the DoctorVOX website:

DoctorVOX Device

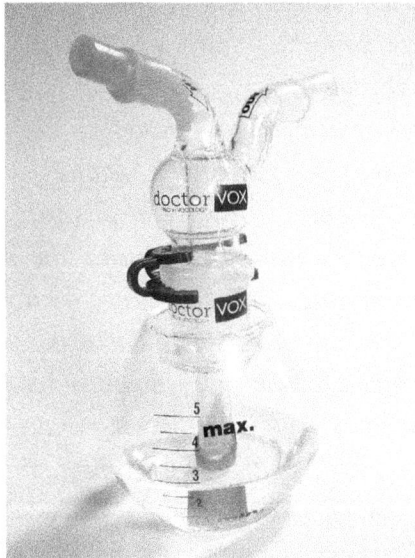

The DoctorVOX device is a new patented device designed to provide voice therapy and vocal

humidification. It is easy to carry and is safe to be used anywhere for vocal habilitation and rehabilitation. So it is intended to assist voice therapy and to serve as a supporting device for professional voice users. DoctorVOX is designed to help motor learning and cognitive processes involved in voice therapy and vocal training. DoctorVOX provides instant humidification of the vocal folds. Additionally, herbal and medical products can also be used for inhalation.

DoctorVOX mainly uses the mechanisms of SOVT and resonance tube exercises for voice therapy and professional voice development. The main mechanism involves artificial elongation of the vocal tract by a built-in tube, and the back pressure is provided by bubbling water and a valve. Elongation and back pressure measures are adjustable for individualization. It is designed for rehabilitation of dysphonic patients and habilitation of the professional voice users.

There are two tube openings on the top. The swan-neck like tube indicates the breathing outlet from the container. There is a valve at this part by which the back pressure can be increased. The phonation inlet is the opening of the inner tube from which the user can blow voice into water. The upper part of the device is formed by two tubes mounted one inside the other. The inner tube is for blowing and phonation. The active length of the inner tube (adjustable) is about the same length with the human vocal tract so that standing waves form in a natural way.

The bottom part of the device (container) is filled with water (to a certain level) for voice therapy exercises. Maximum water height is designed to be below phonation threshold pressure. Water spillage during blowing and aspiration of water during inhalation are prevented by two main mechanisms. First resistance to keep water in container during bubbling is the circle fold (like an ink stand) at the roof of the container. The second resistance is the enlargement in the neck part of the device.

DoctorVOX can also be used as an instant vocal fold humidifier. The user can humidify the vocal folds by inhaling water vapor (40-45°C/104-113°F) through the swan-neck shaped breathing tube. Herbal/medical products are able to be vaporized through bubbling and can be inhaled from breathing tube. During vocal exercise, user blows air/voice through the inner tube and takes the advantages of the physical factors mentioned above. During inhalation from the breathing outlet, air enters from the phonation inlet and passes through water to be humidified. The humidified air directly affects vocal fold mucosa.

There are also advanced versions of the DoctorVOX device. On why these devices were necessary, Dr. Denizoglu states,

Necessity is the mother of invention. After numerous uses of the DoctorVOX glass device, a necessity for adjustable back pressure has appeared. So a Teflon valve was added to the inhalation end of the device. This advanced device was named, VOXelite.

Another necessity was to obtain a device similar to VOXelite that is unbreakable. So, a new compact

version was devised which is manufactured from a glass-like material and has all accessories of the new back pressure valve within. The new unbreakable device was named, VOXpro. With the VOXpro, the users are able to adjust the back pressure level by a knob on the valve. As well, you do not need a special transport bag (since the VOXpro is not breakable like glass) and mounting the accessories (including the maskVOX, Schloemlicher's inhalator, and a length-adjustment tube) is done easily.

Now let's review the VOXelite and VOXpro:

VOXelite

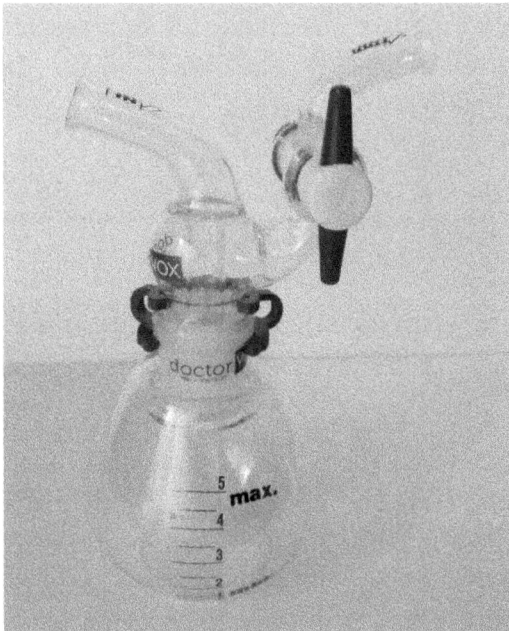

The VOXelite is made of a hygienic glass material. The glass surface is stiffer than traditional silicone

and non-BPA plastic materials, therefore creates more vibration than silicone and plastic. The VOXelite has the same properties as the DoctorVOX Voice Therapy Device, with an additional valve on the inhalation side of the device that allows the user to change the back pressure level easily. By adjusting the newly added back pressure valve, the user can achieve a higher level of back pressure for a more intense therapy session and workout.

VOXpro

The VOXpro is made of Tritan non-BPA plastic material. Tritan does not have a "stiff" surface like glass, thus produces less vibration.. However, the

material has more resistance to cracking. The VOXpro has the same shape as the DoctorVOX Voice Therapy Device and VOXelite, with an additional valve on the inhalation side of the device that allows the user to change the back pressure level easily. By adjusting the newly added back pressure valve, the user can achieve a higher level of back pressure for a more intense therapy session.

Both products have the same properties as a DoctorVOX device:

- *The upper part of each device is formed by two tubes mounted one inside the other; one tube for exhalation and phonation, the other tube for inhalation.*

- *The swan-neck like tube indicates the breathing outlet from the container. The phonation inlet is the opening of the inner tube from which the user can blow into and use the voice for phonation into water. The active length of the inner tube is the same length as the human vocal tract so that standing waves form in a natural way.*

- *The bottom part of the device which is named the container is filled with water for voice therapy exercises. Maximum water height is designed to be below phonation threshold pressure.*

- *Water spillage during blowing and aspiration of water during inhalation, are prevented by two main mechanisms. First resistance to keep water in container during bubbling is the circle fold (like an inkstand) at the roof of the container. The second resistance is the enlargement in the neck part of the device.*

- *The device can also be used as an instant vocal fold humidifier. The user can humidify the vocal folds by inhaling water vapor (40-45°C) through the swan-neck shaped breathing tube. Herbal/medicinal products are able to be vaporized through bubbling and can be inhaled from the breathing tube.*

- *During vocal exercise, the user blows air/voice through the inner tube and takes the advantages of DoctorVox technique. During inhalation from the breathing outlet, air enters from the phonation inlet and passes through water to be humidified. The humidified air directly affects vocal fold mucosa.*

pocketVOX

The pocketVOX Voice Therapy and Vocal Training Tool, which is being used in DoctorVOX Technique, is made of medical grade silicone. It is elastic and its length is 28 cm (11 inches), internal diameter is 9 mm (0.35 inches), and external diameter is 13 mm (0.5 inches). During application, the pocketVOX pen-tip must be dipped into 2-5 cm (0.79-1.97 inches) deep water in a drinking bottle. (You can fit pocketVOX to a 500 cc [16.9 ounce] plastic water plastic bottle neck that you can easily get from any market.) Depth of water changes from exercise to exercise. In the first step, 2 cm (approx. 0.8 inches) depth could be enough. Later on, the depth could be increased according to the therapist's directions.

maskVOX

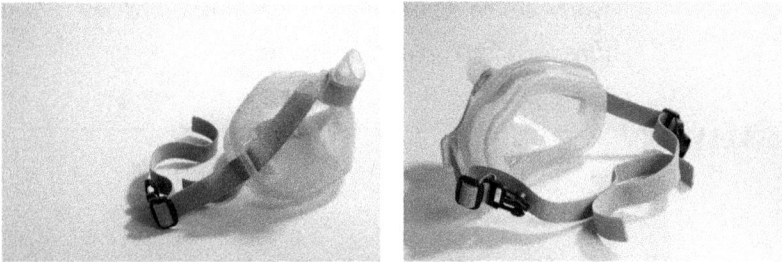

The maskVOX device is to provide free articulation during DoctorVOX Voice Therapy Technique. maskVOX is easily connected to pocketVOX and DoctorVOX devices. The artificial elongation of the vocal tract and back pressure is the physical basis of the DVT. The maskVOX can be used in the treatment of voice and speech disorders. maskVOX is also a supportive device for singers, singing students, and professional voice users. maskVOX is intended

to be a therapeutic tool in singing voice therapy as well.

bottleVOX

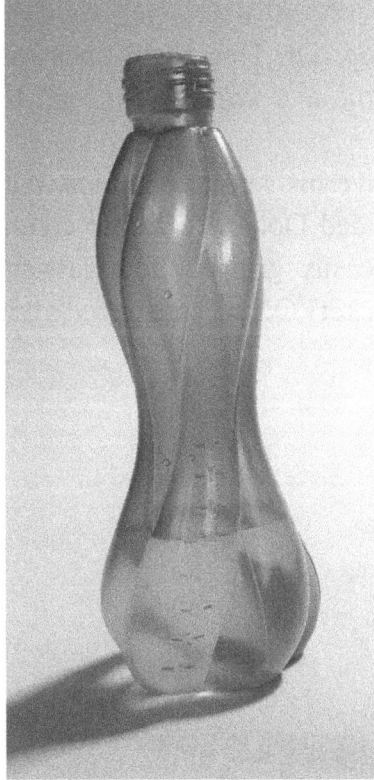

The bottleVOX is made of non BPA plastic, specifically designed with opposing threads for an air-tight fit, which means a pocketVOX must be "pressed" not "screwed" onto a bottleVOX. The hourglass shape assures an easy grip. This original version of the bottleVOX, which was designed at Jaime's request, specifically for the DoctorVOX Vocal Strength Training kit, was based on a mathematical design, which makes it specific for you.

The Fibonacci series and the golden ratio were used. The bottleVOX design contains five (fifth element of Fibonacci series) golden (each 135 degrees turn) spirals on the bottle. The ratios of the general scale are also in golden number Pi.

In a workshop, Dr. Denizoglu once said, *"So what does the shape of this bottle do to help your singing? Absolutely nothing; I just like math."*

Hahaha, I love his sense of humor. All in all, I'm very happy that I prodded DoctorVOX into creating this bottle for me. Having an easily gripped hourglass-shaped bottle that perfectly fits a pocketVOX has answered all my concerns.

Lax Vox Tube

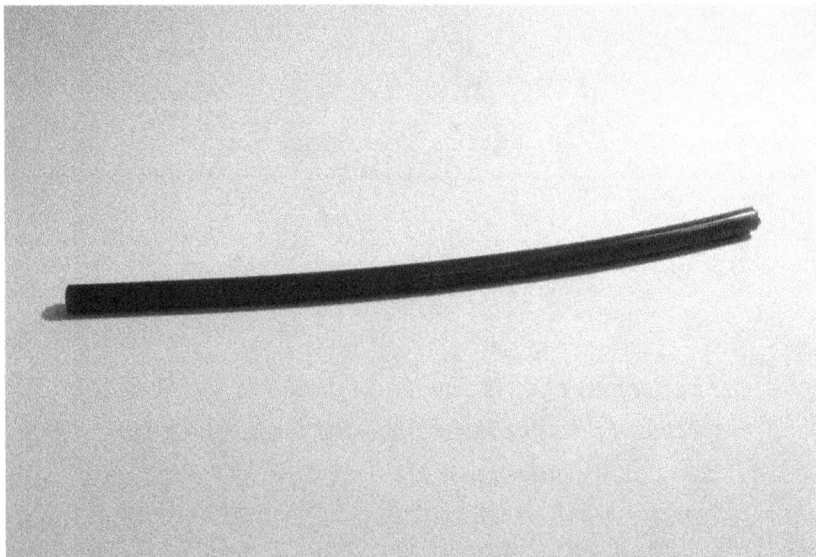

The LaxVox tube is a medical grade silicone tube that is 35 cm (13.8 inches) in length, 10 mm (0.4 inches) inner diameter, and 13 mm (0.5 inches)

outside diameter.

Instead of running to Lowes to buy tubing, I use DoctorVOX Lax Vox tubes, because the end that goes into the bottle has jagged teeth to prevent the blockage of breath release into the water bottle through the end submerged in water. In tubes with no teeth, air pressure becomes blocked when the tube is pressed against the bottom of a bottle of water. Please note that the Lax Vox tube is optional and does not come with the DoctorVOX Vocal Strength Training kit, but can be purchased at DoctorVOX.US.

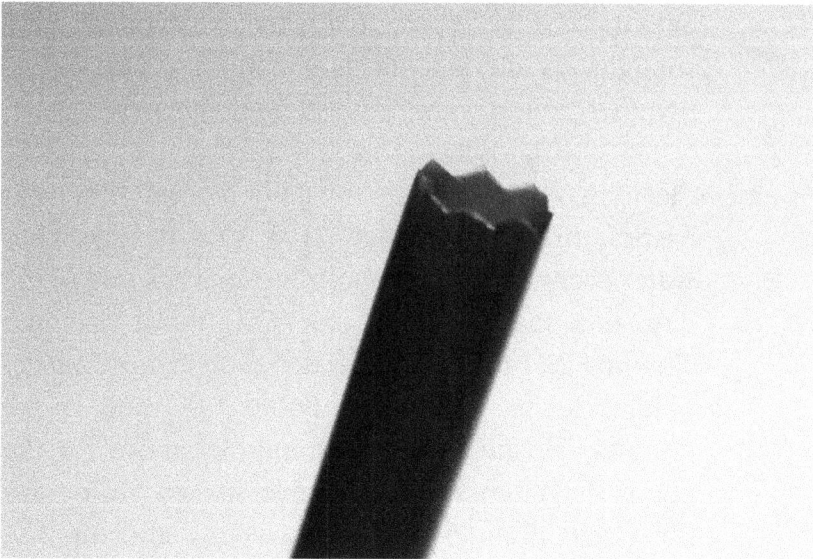

DoctorVOX Tools

Cleaning and Maintenance
Before moving on, it is HIGHLY important that we cover cleaning and maintenance of your DoctorVOX tools in order to increase the lifespan of your tools and keep you healthy.

While DoctorVOX uses non BPA medical-grade silicone and high-grade plastic, any item that you put to your mouth can become a breeding surface for bacteria. As well, silicone and plastic will fade in color, even deteriorate to the point that the surface becomes dull and chalky. Normally, this takes many, many months, but that time frame can become shortened when your DoctorVOX Vocal Strength Training kit is not protected from extreme weather conditions and cleaned thoroughly

Therefore,

#1– It is wise to keep your DoctorVOX tools out of extreme heat, especially when combined with sunlight. While silicone will naturally fade on its own, we do not want to speed up the process.

#2– Cleaning of your devices is a daily process to prevent bacteria from spreading! ALWAYS change your water every day! Empty your water at the end of the day and soak your DoctorVOX Vocal Strength Training kit in hot, soapy water. You can use a baby bottle cleaner for your bottleVOX and small cleaning brushes used for smoothie straws for the pocketVOX tubes. After you've soaked your tools for a few minutes, clean thoroughly and air dry. Refill your water only when ready to use your DoctorVOX Vocal Strength Training kit.

This is generally all that is needed, however many may prefer a full bacteria cleanse.

Vendera Vocal Academy associate, and co-creator of the Fellow Songwriters Workshop, Claude LaRoche prefers a deep cleaning by using a bleach solution. Claude says,

"Any device in contact with saliva is considered contaminated and presents a health hazard. Period. Bacteria may proliferate over a relatively short period of time. They can even be seen with the naked eye as they colonized. They appear as black dots.

Your DoctorVOX Vocal Strength Training kit should be clean and sanitized. By the way, rubbing alcohol, peroxide, and household cleaning products are not indicated as disinfectants for this purpose.

I clean the pocketVOX using the same method we used a few years back to clean CPR mannequins after training sessions. We had thousands and thousands of people giving mouth to mouth to those dummies. So it had to be safe. This method is derived from Dr. Dakin, a surgeon who developed a solution to clean soldier's wounds during the first Great War. The active ingredient in Dr. Dakin's solution is simply household bleach.

Here is the procedure:

Right after a session, IMMEDIATELY sanitize your devices.

Rinse thoroughly the device under running water. If you are using a maskVOX, open the double lip with your fingers and make sure water is running over every single surface of the mask. Use a small brush if necessary.

Prepare the bleach based solution. The proportion is one tablespoon of bleach per liter of water. This solution is not stabilized so you need to prepare it from scratch each time.

Submerge completely the device in the solution for 20 minutes. Make sure every single surface of the device is in contact with the solution.

Rinse thoroughly under running water to remove any solution left on the device.

Let the device dry by itself.

Don't increase the proportion of bleach in the solution. Always rinse thoroughly. Bleach residue may burn or irritate the skin around your mouth (maskVOX) or your lips (pocketVOX). Don't forget to sanitize the bottle you are using. Do not share the device during a session."

I must admit, I had never cleaned my tools this thoroughly until Claude shared his procedure. Now I will use this process daily.

Now that you're familiar with each device, we will move to the exercises. Please note that while I own and use a glass DoctorVOX device, I generally use a pocketVOX and bottleVOX for all of my vocal therapy exercises and when teaching my students how to perform Isolation exercises with these tools. Regardless, you can interchange the tools with every exercise explained.

CHAPTER FOUR
— *Rebalancing Therapy* —

Now that you understand the basic principles and are familiar with the DoctorVOX tools, it's time for the exercises.

I will present the remainder of the book in two training regimens:

1. My vocal therapy routine as prescribed by Dr. Denizoglu.

2. "Vocal Weightlifting" routines for those who prefer to use DoctorVOX devices with the Isolation exercises explained in my books and at Vendera Vocal Academy.

Let's start with my "rebalancing" therapy sessions to show you how Dr. Denizoglu prescribed a routine specific to my voice type and vocal issue.

Before we dive into the training, I want to note one more time that this is NOT a book on DVT therapy. We WILL cover the few DVT exercises that Dr. Denizoglu chose for my therapy sessions, but we will focus on using DoctorVOX devices with Isolation exercises from my own methodology in the next chapter.

Regardless of which routine you choose, a few rules must be followed when using DoctorVOX devices:

1. When vocalizing, maintain a lowered larynx. The easiest way to keep the larynx lowered when using a pocketVOX or DoctorVOX device is to think, "Uh,"

as in "glove," to create a low/neutral laryngeal position while you slide through your vocal range.

2. If you hear any breath escaping as you vocalize, you're letting air escape from around your lips, and/or the seal from the pocketVOX to the bottle is not tight enough. If you have a bottleVOX and not a regular water bottle, the seal will be tight so that no air escapes. If you're using another water bottle, check the seal of the bottle by holding the pocketVOX and shaking the water bottle up and down. If the bottle slips off the pocketVOX, the seal isn't tight enough— and you'll spill water everywhere, ha-ha, so I suggest you try this over a sink. If the seal is tight but you still hear air, reposition your lips for a better seal.

3. The sound of your voice and the visual sight of bubbles must happen simultaneously.

4. If you can hear your voice first, before you see bubbles in the water, it means *you are using a hard attack; you are creating a vocal burst followed by air.*

5.   If you see the bubbles first, before you hear your voice, it means *you are starting with a soft or breathy attack; air passes between vocal folds before they vibrate.*

When all falls into place, exercising with DoctorVOX devices will result in:

- A *relaxed, lowered larynx*
- *More efficient thyroarytenoid (TA) muscle for better muscle involvement*
- *More resonating volume from vocal tract elongation*
- *Larynx/hyoid bone/tongue relation loosens, and the tongue*

moves forward

- *Excess neck and shoulder tension decreases*

- *Correct breathing habits (lower abdominal/diaphragmatic breathing as explained in* Raise Your Voice*) becomes natural*

- *Lowered airflow*

- *Less effort in voice production*

These are but a few of the benefits of using DoctorVOX devices.

Let's start where I began in my sessions with Dr. Denizoglu, finding my primal sound. Remember from our definitions that the primal sound is your raw, true sound. It sounds like a caveman voicing "uh" to make his/her emotions known to others.

Primal Sound

Once Dr. Denizoglu knew I had my primal sound, we focused on opening the pharynx above the cords so that I didn't "clamp" the vocal cords shut. To assure this wouldn't happen, Dr. Denizoglu taught me the Muttley laugh, which, as you already know, is a reference to a beloved cartoon character dog.

This is a silent laugh (without pitch) but you'll obviously hear air pass through the cords. This allows you to feel those false vocal folds opening. A split second before I make this type of laugh, those FVFs open, as in a pre-yawn position.

Once I understood this, I of course applied correct technique (breathing, support, and placement) and initialized my primal sound by taking what I call a micro-breath on a

yawn, which is the easiest way to open the false vocal folds. When I told Dr. Denizoglu about the micro-breath on a yawn, he said,

> *Your method is a good combination, which is also used in classical pedagogy and often referred to using the "fish smile" or the pre-yawn position, which mimics the face you make during a bad smell.*

This is the basis for your sound production. Refer to the videos for further guidance. Now I will explain what exercises I do for DVT therapy, starting with my personal warmup routine.

The pocketVOX/Voice RX Warmup

The pocketVOX/*Voice RX Warmup* is a unique warmup routine. While Dr. Denizoglu did not guide me on this part, he did say that the pocketVOX is a great warmup tool. Therefore, I use my pocketVOX with my *Voice RX Warmup* mp3 instead of performing lip bubbles as the warmup requires.

Dr. Denizoglu has each patient use the pocketVOX or DoctorVOX device multiple times per day, whether it is one minute every hour or for longer periods multiple times per day, depending on how dedicated each individual is. This part he left up to me, which is why I chose to use the pocketVOX with my own *Voice RX Warmup* mp3. I've been doing this for several years and always within 30 minutes after waking up.

Before I had a bottleVOX, I used any water bottle filled one-half to two-thirds full of water. But upon my last private vocal examination with Dr. Denizoglu, I discovered I was using way too much water (more on adjusting water levels later), which was creating too much back pressure, or, "too much weight on the voice." I've since adjusted my water levels to a much lower level to assure I applied less weight on my voice.

Now I start with very little water in the bottle, generally at 8 to 9 on the pocketVOX tube markings or 3 to 4 on the bottleVOX.

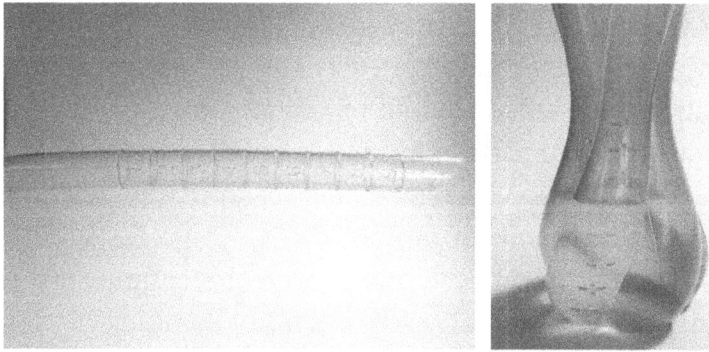

The *Voice RX Warmup* is 15 minutes long, so it's the perfect length for an adequate SOVT-type warmup. Again, I also perform this warmup every morning within 30 minutes after waking and typically on my way to the gym, which is 15 minutes from my house.

After warming up (and finishing at the gym), I move right into my main therapy exercise, Dr. Denizoglu's Corridor exercise.

The Corridor Exercise via 10,000 Challenge

Dr. Denizoglu's main therapy exercise for me was the Corridor exercise. At its core, this is a basic Siren slide from low to high, just like we cover in *Raise Your Voice*, with one major difference—the slide must start in full voice and smoothly transition into a mixed voice tone, even into falsetto at the extreme high part of my range.

In all honesty, this exercise was EXTREMELY hard for me.

Why?

Dr. Denizoglu said,

Because you know too much.

Hahaha, what a response. But it's true. Knowing the inner workings of voice strengthening made it difficult for me to let go of certain muscular tensions and allow my tone to transition from full voice into mixed into falsetto, when I was so accustomed to performing Sirens in full voice only. But, by learning to do so, I could better balance the relationship between the TA and CT muscles.

In my situation, I've been overcompensating by over-tensing my TA muscles, even when not speaking or singing, so it makes perfect sense why this exercise was so challenging for me. And don't be fooled, it is still challenging for me.

So, what is the Corridor exercise? Before I explain it, allow Dr. Denizoglu to explain why it's called the "Corridor exercise":

The Corridor exercise combines several skills simultaneously: keeping a comfortably low larynx during high notes, controlling the FVFs by preventing the trying hard reflex, activating the CT muscle dominantly for elevating the pitch, and engaging abdominodiaphragmatic support at the same time.

This exercise at its core is a vocal slide from low to high back to low. Please note that as you slide into your higher notes it is not an empty (naive) and breathy falsetto sound. With that said, the comfortable low falsetto can be used to find the way in the beginning.

In the first few weeks, the trainee is supposed to acquire the skill, then transfer it into performance. When everything has settled, it is really a luxury at stage to execute, without thinking how to hit the high note. Like playing an instrument: the note is already THERE, to go and take it easily.

Here is a brief explanation of how to perform the Corridor exercise:

First you need to be aware of what you are feeling during those high notes; negative exercise helps a lot to find the correct feeling. The negative exercise is to make (and exaggerate) the thing that you are not supposed to do. In our case, this would be constricting the voice so you may understand what you are not supposed to do.

Next, for the negative exercise, you try to "push the sound" up into a narrow place. Pushing the sound up means to travel (push up and make it more constricted!) in the corridor which goes up feeling as if it is narrowing so that you can physically feel what you do. This aims to increase the awareness of what you are doing, which is the opposite way of what we want you to do.

Once you've connected to this constriction, we must feel the opposite, or the correct way. You must start the corridor again, but this time as the corridor narrows, you must maintain the sensation of open FVFs, and then try to feel the large and light corridor down as you continue sliding up in your range.

In other words, the top notes are felt in the lower-front turn of the corridor. Please note that when done correctly, it is not a pushy feeling, yet is not totally effortless; you need a great deal of focus and effort, especially for the high notes. But this effort is about "opening" the FVFs, not closing, or pushing, or trying hard. The sound quality is also relaxed, without breathiness in voice and easy to produce. But again, it is not totally effortless; we need a delicate control and effort to open the FVFs.

If you're having trouble, you can start with a low falsetto and take it to chest. Regardless of your initial tone, don't worry about the break at the beginning. Just make sure that you feel as if the low pitches are placed in the corridor behind your nape of the neck. By feeling the sound corridor beginning behind the neck on the low notes, you are provided a few opportunities:

1. *You control the CT relaxation by the opposite support of PCA (the posterior cricoarytenoid muscle, which opens the glottis).*

2. *You control the vertical larynx position (comfortably low larynx position).*

3. *You do not push the larynx for the low tones (you know the typical position: the chin is dropped down, pushed onto the sternum, the face mimics emotions such as suffering, etc.).*

Refer to the following pictures to visualize how the corridor comes into play from the low pitches to high pitches all within the structure of our neck, pharynx, and mouth:

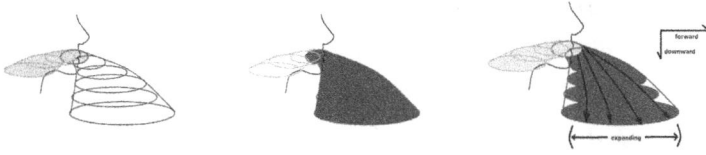

Jaime had a lot of questions when I worked with him in therapy sessions. He often wondered if I meant that we must "squeeze" the FVFs as we start this exercise and if there were a noticeable tonal change from full voice to falsetto. So, to clarify, since many of you use his methodology from Raise Your Voice, *yes, you can indeed start from chest (full) as you ascend to the high notes OR choose to start with a low falsetto if you're having trouble at first ascending into the high notes. But, when you are in the corridor, it is better to think more of the mixed voice instead of thinking of chest voice or full voice or head voice or falsetto; simply think of a mixed tone.*

The gear system of the larynx is now "automatic" (in the corridor) instead of manual, which means that for nearly one and a half to two octaves (something like between A3-F5) you will have a stable timbre. There will be no breaks and no different timbres (full or false).

Over and below these borders, you generally use more and more dominance of TA for below, and CT for upper tones. In other words, below A3 it becomes more chesty and above F5 it becomes more falsetty.

It is better to start from the mouth sensation (palate buzz on your bottom starting pitch, which is generally around A3-D4) after finding the primal sound as long as you can manage to keep the pathway forward-down as you ascend to the high tones. If not, you'll flip into falsetto, which is generally an unused "device" and managed to be produced by reflexes in the modal register.

For the record, falsetto is a tone we generally don't use in our everyday lives when we speak, so it is not loaded by personal, emotional, or environmental stress and so has not been affected like our true voice.

So, yes, I DO mention about the negative exercise in reference to the FVF contraction (not for trying hard, which is a contraction to midline, but for opening to sides as in an open throat as in Muttley laugh, as then in the pre-yawn position) so that the singer can understand the complete opposite of "trying hard."

It is not easy to feel the FVFs. One can feel it better during the "trying hard" contractions. So first, when learning this exercise, feel the sensation of the FVFs being closed, and then immediately feel the opposite (the Muttley) as the FVFs open during the pre-yawn on a silent laugh; and then try to control the degree of opening and closing the FVFs.

Just to clarify once more, the "trying hard sensation" is the opposite of the yawn. When trying hard, we increase the valve force on the FVFs for closure and squeeze. During pre-yawn (Jaime's micro-breath on a yawn, the fish smile, etc.) the FVFs are forced to open. Our goal is to "try" not to "try hard" if possible whenever we are in the corridor, thus the purpose of the pre-yawn.

With that said, it is possible to squeeze when applying some tonal ornaments such as grit (it is not an illegal issue). In this instance, the effort is to close the FVF valve. However, the effort to sing in the forward-down corridor is the effort of opening the FVFs. This is why we close the valve for an instant and then open the valve as we sing; to learn to maintain open FVFs.

When performing the Corridor exercise, there is no need to use an mp3, or Tuned XD, a pitch wheel, or a keyboard, because this exercise simply requires you to slide from low to high back to low with no real thought about your beginning or ending note.

This makes the Corridor exercise a perfect candidate for a 10,000 Challenge. For those of you in the Vendera Vocal Academy and those who have read my book *PractiSING,* you'll recall that a 10,000 Challenge is simply the act of performing 10,000 repetitions of any given vocal exercise.

When performing a 10,000 Challenge, you can use a pitch counter to keep track of your reps. What's a pitch counter? It's a little clicker counter that goes from 0000 to 9,999. I have one hanging around my wrist on the front cover of this book. You can also use a clicker counter app on your smartphone. I actually have a clicker app on my Apple Watch.

I do my Corridor exercise slides starting as low as comfortable in my range and then sliding as high as comfortable and back down, always focused on sliding from full voice right into a mixed tone while in the "corridor," even up into falsetto at the very top and back into full voice. I also pay close attention to the corridor illustrations in this book.

The more repetitions that I perform in one workout session, the larger my range becomes, my lower end lowering and my higher end going higher.

However, with my damage, I do have a muscular

imbalance that I notice mostly right around G4 above my first break and again at G5 that results in a weird falsetto flip, but it is slowly correcting itself because I also lock onto the vowel for focus.

"What vowel?" you ask.

A whole lotta "whoas!"

Dr. Denizoglu has me sliding on "WHOA." The "W" prevents me from creating a breathy attack or a glottal shock, and the "oh" vowel, as in "tow," helps to keep my larynx lowered. He also prefers that my transition into falsetto at the very top stays in "low falsetto" so that my larynx remains low.

"What about that 'uh' you mentioned earlier?"

The "uh," as in "glove," is more of a mental anchor to help maintain a lowered larynx. So, while I am singing "Whoa," I am thinking "uh."

You'll recall from our earlier definitions that a low (larynx) falsetto has a darker, hootier sound, while a high (larynx) falsetto has a thinner, brighter, edgier sound.

Since I had so much trouble in the beginning, not being able to smoothly transition from full voice to mixed voice to falsetto, my first 10,000 Challenge was a bit different. I modified Dr. Denizoglu's "prescription" for me and broke the slides down as follows to keep me working from full voice to falsetto:

1. One pocketVOX slide

2. One Microbubble slide

3. One pocketVOX slide

4. One "ooo" slide

5. One pocketVOX slide

6. Two "whoa" slides

This meant I had to do seven slides to complete a set. This became my "seven-rep routine." The first five reps made it easier for me to slide right into mixed voice and then into falsetto with no breaks, especially on the "ooo" vowel (as in the word "food"). Placing a pocketVOX slide between the other reps helped to maintain the muscle memory balance I gained from the back pressure, I repeated the "whoa" slide twice because it was my main exercise.

I've had many students perform similar 10,000 Challenges with great success. Touring singers like James LaBrie (Dream Theater) and Brian Burkheiser (I Prevail) noticed great benefit from a basic 10,000 Challenge with the pocketVOX slide alone.

Exercises with DoctorVOX devices are a staple in my teaching practice especially when working with private students that come to my studio at My Place Productions in Columbus, Ohio...and all of my students eventually face a 10,000 Challenge.

For example, my student Carl Wyatt has been working on a version of my seven-rep routine for a 10,000 Challenge. Since Carl's job has him behind the wheel most if his day, he performs hundreds of slides on the road. He told me that it was easy to lose track when he alternated the exercises because he cannot click his clicker while driving, so he keeps track in his head.

I told Carl that he could simplify his routine in order to keep better track by doing ten slides of each type instead of doing one rep of each exercise.

So, if you're interested in performing this 10,000 Challenge but find it easier to perform ten pocketVOX slides, then ten Microbubble slides, etc., feel free to change the routine as needed. Your voice will still benefit!

Modified 10,000 Challenge

After I finished my first seven-rep routine 10,000 Challenge, I switched strictly to pocketVOX and "Whoa" slides, and I will complete ten thousand 10,000 Challenges if necessary. All in all, I perform anywhere from 100 to 250 slides per day.

E-Scream Slides

The E-scream slide was a second therapy exercise that Dr. Denizoglu gave me to help strengthen my CT muscles by using a high falsetto sound. He demonstrated this exercise (which I've already used before) on random pitches during one of our Skype sessions. I actually practice this exercise in a methodical manner so that I can work from tenor C to soprano A. I make sure to stick to the high falsetto tone for a brighter sound, although I DO focus on a lowered larynx. You *can* still have a brighter falsetto without raising the larynx up too high; it just takes practice.

For this exercise, a 10,000 Challenge need not apply. I use my Tuned XD app to do this exercise, using a preprogrammed scale that completes a full mini-Siren slide in thirds, starting at C5 and working up to F5. This means my first mini-Siren goes C5-E5-C5 and my last slide goes F5-A5-F5.

E-Scream Slides

Yes, the last three slides of my Tuned XD scale have been challenging, even frustrating at times, considering that I regularly belted out soprano As and up to soprano C sharp, and even found soprano D (D6 not in whistle voice) multiple times. But I am diligent and patient, and I know I will rebalance those muscular coordinations and make my CT muscles stronger!

My Singing Routine

Ah, singing, the reason we all got into this in the first place. Unfortunately, I'd forgotten that was my reason only a few years back. Dealing with vocal pain can sway you away from what you truly love. Even before my accident, my daily singing had become limited, my job as vocal coach taking precedence. While I understand that I need to work, I must remember that I need to sing.

I recall a conversation I had with vocal coach/singer, Daniel Formica (YourVocalTeacher.com) several years ago. Daniel was telling me that he was having some minor vocal issues. It was nothing serious, but he felt that his stamina wasn't as prominent as it had been. We chatted for a bit, and a few months later, when we had another conversation, he told me he had fixed his issue—by singing!

You see, Daniel realized that he wasn't singing regularly, but once he started singing for over an hour every day, he found his vocal spark once again.

Ironically, I literally had a dream about Daniel one night. It woke me up because he was screaming at me in the dream, yelling that I needed to get off my lazy butt and start singing every day to get my own vocal spark back.

I heeded his words, even messaged him to whine because he ripped me hard in my dreams, hahaha. I'm sure he smiled and giggled because he said he was glad to help.

So, my daily routine has returned, but I've started very slow. Over the past two and a half months I've went from one song per day to five songs per day. I've made a commitment to add one new song to sing every day every two weeks, with my goal to reach a minimum of 16 songs.

Basically, my original vision was to go from a three-minute daily singing routine to nearly 90 minutes of daily singing. It has been tough to stick to my routine because any given day my voice may be in disarray from my nerve damage. But, I will prevail and by month eight, I will be a singing machine once again!

Some of the songs I've chosen are covers, but the majority of my work comes from singing my own originals from my own projects, such as songs for my *Extreme Scream* series, Vendera & Stith, and my favorite band project, Angel Fire East (with Ryan Wall).

Ironically, Angel Fire East was born out of my therapy sessions. I'd forgotten how much I loved singing in falsetto, that haunting tone used by artists like Prince, and the light, ethereal tones of singers like Amy Lee (Evanescence) until I started hammering away at the Corridor exercise.

An important note to add is that I sing these songs using my maskVOX attached to my pocketVOX. (I will explain more later.)

Bottom line, being a little stricter with my training schedule (albeit at a snail's crawl pace) has helped me find my love of singing again!

That, my singing friends, is my simple therapy routine: warming up daily via the *Voice RX Warmup* with a pocketVox, a 10,000 Challenge for the Corridor exercise, one daily session of the E-Scream slides, and singing.

But, I'd be remiss if I didn't share with you another effective therapy technique that can only be performed on my voice by Dr. Denizoglu as my physician—shiatsu of the voice.

Shiatsu of the Voice

I would be presenting a disservice to you if I did not share one of the most important parts of my vocal therapy rehabilitation sessions with Dr. Denizoglu. When he examined me, he also performed what is called "shiatsu of the voice," which is essentially a massage of the throat on various pressure points.

I cannot perform this technique on myself, because I could literally black out if I applied pressure to the wrong points. Shiatsu of the voice is a series of palpation and press/release techniques that were performed directly on my pharyngeal wall as well as on my neck around my larynx.

I've had three sessions with Dr. Denizoglu so far, and the knot that was once the size of a large marble has shrunk to the size of a pea. My last session had Dr. Denizoglu sweating. He'd noticed that my larynx had shifted out of center alignment to the side of my throat. In other words, my larynx was no longer centered, but pulled out of alignment in the front of my neck by excess muscle tension in my TA muscles.

Regarding my situation, he said,

> *Phonatory habits can be affected by many domino effects on the body and soul. To my opinion, after you have had the glass in your throat, it behaved like a small stone in your left shoe. You felt it at every step and tried to compensate for the feeling by using your muscles in a different manner, which caused muscular strain, weakness, and imbalance. This is how we transfer the compensations into behaviours in life.*

I treasure these sessions, which are few and far

between—he lives and practices in Turkey, while I live in the United States. But I am sure we will be conducting vocal workshops together, and I'll gladly be paid in shiatsu sessions, hahaha.

I'm sure I piqued your interest, so feel free to ask your ENT if he/she is familiar with shiatsu of the voice.

Now that you've had a view of what my DVT therapy session looks like, it's time to look at how I personally use DoctorVOX tools with my own students in conjunction with my Isolation exercises. Let's move on.

CHAPTER FIVE

— The DoctorVOX Vocal Strength

Training Kit—

(And a Few Bonus Tips)

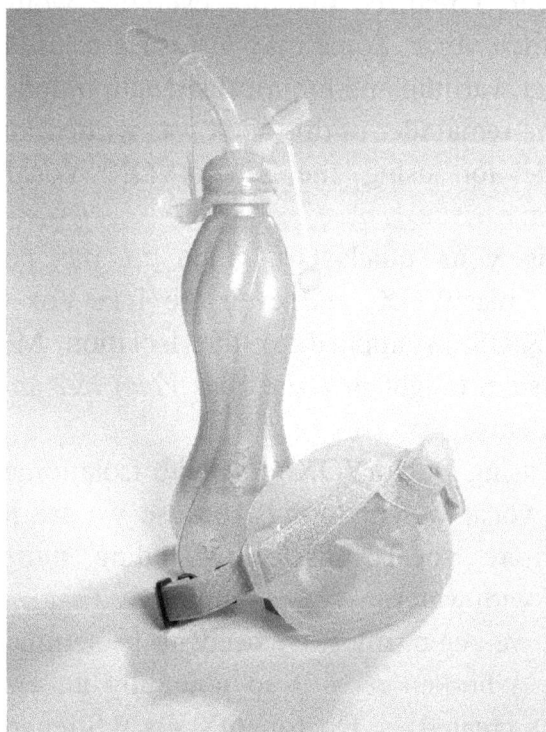

The idea for this book actually started out as a booklet to help singers apply my exercises with the new DoctorVOX Vocal Strength Training kit, which was created for me for DoctorVOX.US. The DoctorVOX Vocal Strength Training kit is the official, clear-colored "Vendera" version of a pocketVOX, maskVOX, and bottleVOX in a three-piece kit.

It was my intention to write a basic booklet for the DoctorVOX Vocal Strength Training kit to describe how I wanted my students to use these tools when performing my Isolation exercises. But then I felt an urge to share my personal story in hopes that those of you who are dealing with vocal issues, such as nodules, bowed cords, or muscle tension dysphonia, would find new hope in knowing that you can overcome your vocal issues—that you could "rebalance your voice."

However, I realized that not everyone would need to rebalance their voice. Some may just want to use these tools for a quicker warmup and for vocal strength training. If this is the case, the remainder of this book was written for you. It is THE guide for using the DoctorVOX Vocal Strength Training kit.

This is your quick-start guide to the pocketVOX, bottleVOX, maskVOX, and even the Lax Vox tube from DoctorVOX.US as applied to the Isolation Method, the exercise system taught in *Raise Your Voice 1&2* and Vendera Vocal Academy.

When using DoctorVOX tools with Isolation exercises, I liken it to vocal weight lifting, because we are focused on building more vocal muscle by adding more "weight resistance" with water.

Before we begin, my story needs to be summed up once again (like a broken record) so you fully understand why DoctorVOX created the DoctorVOX Vocal Strength Training kit for me and why it is so important to you as a singer. Besides, I know many of you skipped the beginning of this book to jump right into vocal weightlifting. So, the following few pages are "broken record" repeats, which you can skim, speed read, or whatever you have to do, but take it all in before moving on. Let's proceed.

In the past few years, humming through straws has become all the rage with singers and vocal coaches. Personally, I didn't find humming through a straw as relaxing for my throat as I had when humming into a sink full of water through an aquarium tube. People were humming through regular-sized soda straws, large straws, even very tiny coffee straws. In fact, I noticed that many singers and coaches were pushing coffee straws as a fix-it-all tool for vocal issues.

While I am not trying to argue the benefit of a coffee straw or dissuade you from using one, I felt that such a tiny straw was causing too much back pressure, leading to constriction and strain, so I did not use them with my students. In addition, without humming through a straw into water, I didn't feel it was as effective for creating the vibrational effect of the back pressure upon the vocal cords and surrounding muscles.

Recalling my "humming into an aquarium tube in a sink full of water" days, I purchased some tubing from Lowes home improvement store and tried a 12-inch piece of tubing in a gallon of water. It was a little difficult to carry around, so I decided to switch to a regular water bottle and try a large-diameter rubber straw that people use for smoothies, because the diameter of the larger straw made my voice feel better than a regular-sized straw did.

I didn't notice as much vibration with the rubber straw as I did with a gallon of water, but Dr. Denizoglu assured me that a bottle of water presents just as much a massage effect as a gallon of water. Furthermore, I could slightly bend the rubber straw so that I didn't have to bend my neck down at an angle that would throw the vocal path out of alignment.

Not long after I discovered the DoctorVOX device, Dr. Ilter Denizoglu sent me a DoctorVOX device, and after using the DoctorVOX device for less than an hour, I fell in love with it. It helped me tremendously because I had some serious vocal pain and hoarseness after that small sliver of glass got embedded in the back of my throat during the television show in Tokyo, which resulted in nerve damage.

However, I was concerned that the glass DoctorVOX device wouldn't suit my needs when I was on the road—I was afraid I would break it while traveling to perform on various television shows and when conducting vocal workshops.

So I asked Dr. Denizoglu if he could create a new product that would consist simply of the DoctorVOX mouthpiece made out of plastic or rubber as opposed to glass; something that a singer could fit into their back pocket. I even said that he should name it the pocketVOX.

To my surprise and elation, Dr. Denizoglu did indeed create the pocketVOX. Now that I had this unique vocal tool in my "pocket," so to speak, I began using it throughout the day. It was much easier using a rubber piece in a bottle of water, as opposed to carrying around my DoctorVOX. I also began using it with my students. This little tool began to change my life.

Dealing with vocal nerve damage is not something a singer or coach can deal with lightly, or something I'd wish upon anyone. I wake up with throat irritation daily, have random bouts of hoarseness, I have to spend much more time than usual to warm up my voice, and I have experienced a loss of vocal focus and power at and above soprano G. Finally, at any given moment, my voice can disappear without warning, not returning for minutes, sometimes hours.

Nerves are a funny thing. However, by using the pocketVOX, I began to notice that the nerve pain and swelling in my throat was lessening, if only for a limited amount of time. Regardless, this simple tool had become my main vocal therapy device, and it's guiding me toward the road to recovering from the nerve damage.

The pocketVOX is now a staple in my daily workouts. In fact, it's now a common vocal tool in thousands of singers' lives. Those who know me know that I've been blessed to work with many great singers, such as James LaBrie (Dream Theater), Clayton Stroope (Thriving Ivory), Eric Emery (Starset), Dustin Bates (Starset), Terry Ilous (XYZ), Brian Burkheiser (I Prevail), and Marshal Dutton (Hinder) to name a few. I've made sure that these singers began using pocketVOX, because this simple tool could possibly save their voices on the road and in the studio!

In fact, critically acclaimed rock singer, Tony Harnell said that the pocketVOX is like natural steroids, helping his voice to feel effortless as he sings.

This device is so amazing that I continue to push it to every singer I've ever met, such as Steve Augeri (Journey), Ralf Scheepers (Primal Fear), Ray West (Weapons of Anew/ Spread Eagle), Tom Keifer (Cinderella), Danny Case (From Ashes to New), even well-known Bollywood playback singers and composers (Shalmali Kholgade, Antara Mitra, Harshdeep Kaur, Shannon Donald, Pritam Chakraborty, Vishal Dadlani, Nakash Aziz, Amit Mishra, Sreerama Chandra,), and many more.

Why?

Because the pocketVOX CAN and WILL help to warm up your voice faster and more effectively than any warmup routine on its own. It is an amazing tool for reducing vocal cord swelling when you're hoarse from over-singing, shouting, or sick with a cold. Dr. Denizoglu also uses this therapy tool in conjunction with DVT therapy to reverse vocal cord nodules and help remedy other vocal issues.

So, if the pocketVOX is effective enough to reverse nodules, imagine how amazing your healthy voice will feel once you begin using it!

With all this praise, sadly, you can still only vocalize through a pocketVOX; in other words, you cannot articulate your words, thus no singing.

Which is why Dr. Denizoglu created the maskVOX, a rubber facial mask that can attach to the pocketVOX and DoctorVOX, allowing full articulation on any given vocal exercise and full range of singing words, while receiving the benefits of back pressure.

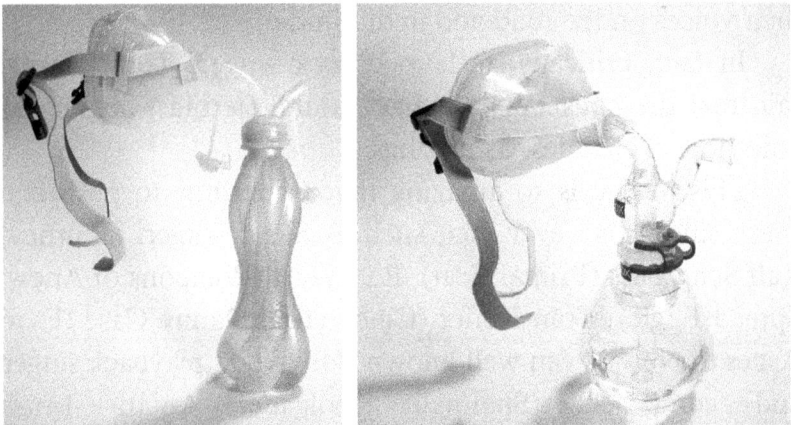

Now I had the best of both worlds! I could attach the maskVOX to my pocketVOX and perform any vocal exercise and sing any song while also bubbling my bottle of water for full back pressure benefits. That means those vocal cords were almost being "vacuumed" together by the back pressure, vibrating themselves to the correct pitches.

What does this mean for a singer?

It means "less involvement of the medial muscles," which are all the muscles around the vocal cords that help you sing. Singers tend to over-squeeze the neck muscles, even using too much muscular tension internally, forcing those tiny vocal cords together and weakening the medial muscles (PCA, TA, and CT muscles). This will only create excess friction and result in vocal strain, hoarseness, or worse, vocal loss that derives from vocal cord inflammation.

But now that we have these amazing tools, we can train our voice to use less muscular involvement while still maintaining full vocal efficiency! Which is why I have worked with DoctorVOX to create the kit known as the DoctorVOX Vocal Strength Training kit. This way, I had a complete training tool kit for my students!

The DoctorVOX Vocal Strength Training kit comes with a pocketVOX, a maskVOX, a bottleVOX, a pdf copy of this book, and the accompanying audio files and instructional videos, which you can access via the Members section.

Following is a breakdown of how I use the DoctorVOX Vocal Strength Training kit with all my students. This is a unique approach to aiding the development of your range, power, and stamina, enabling rapid recovery from a hoarse voice and warming up the voice quicker than ever before.

If you are familiar with my books, products, and websites, such as *Raise Your Voice*, *V24*, and the Vendera Vocal Academy, then these exercises will seem familiar. That's great! You're already one step ahead!

Before diving into the next chapter to learn the exercises, I'd like to offer a few bonus tips, such as adjusting for the best water levels and other ways to use each DoctorVOX training tool.

Adjusting Water Levels

In the beginning, when I first started using these tools, I was filling my water bottle so high that I could barely squeak out a sound. Many times when I did, water shot out of the shorter tube on the pocketVOX. In fact, I've had this happen to students when performing exercises and going a little higher in their range. Yes, I've been splashed many times, hahaha.

What I've learned in private lessons with Dr Denizoglu is that "less is more."

So, when working with a new student who has the bottleVOX, I generally have them start with water around the 2 mark on their bottle. We hum into the bottle, with one hand placed on the front of the throat to see how strong the vibration feels on and in the larynx.

Then we increase the water levels incrementally from 3 to 4 to 5 to see which level of water creates the "best throat vibration" or feels like the best "vocal massage."

You'll notice that the numbers on a bottleVOX run from 1 to 8, with 1 toward the bottom, while the numbers on the pocketVOX run from 1 to 9, with 9 at the bottom closest to the slanted tip opening. If you do not have a bottleVOX and are using a regular water bottle, start testing for the best vocal vibration by starting at number 9 on your pocketVOX to test the vibration, incrementally increasing the water level from 8 up to 7 up to 6.

Please note that more water equals more back pressure for heavier weight for your "vocal weightlifting" workout routine. This is not a test of strength, so do NOT think that having more water in your bottle means you'll get a better vocal muscle workout. Finding the best water level is about finding perfect balance and finding the "best massage." I started at a level of 2 on the bottle and worked up to a 6.

If you're using a DoctorVOX device, you'll notice that the glass bottle is numbered 1 through 5, with 1 at the bottom. I initially started at a water level of 1 and haven't gone any higher than 3-1/2.

Bottom line, find YOUR best level and always adjust the level according to your needs.

Once you connect the maskVOX to the pocketVOX or DoctorVOX, you'll also notice that your "best water level for the best vocal vibration" might suddenly feel off. It might even feel a little tougher to create bubbles. That's because you've changed the "volume" equation. Even air has mass, and now that you are vocalizing through a mask instead of humming directly into a tube, you've added the air mass within the mask.

Generally, you'll need a little less water when attaching a maskVOX. Dr. Denizoglu says,

> *The trick is simple; you will need to decrease the water level when you switch to the maskVOX. You can decide by an empiric way, testing for the best vibration to choose your best water level. Why must we change the water level? Because the air column becomes heavier when attaching the mask (the air in the tube and mask is a mass, not emptiness; so it is a mass that we push in a sense). So it is normal to experience a harder feeling if you do not have a powerful/fit voice as an advanced laxvoxer!*

Adjusting Water Levels

Inhalation Tips

With the inhalation tube on both the DoctorVOX device and pocketVOX, you can inhale warm water (40-50 Celsius/104-122 Fahrenheit) for a more "vocal sauna" sensation. This is why the DoctorVOX device comes with a "thermos," which is essentially a wrap for the DoctorVOX device when using with hot water so you don't burn your hands.

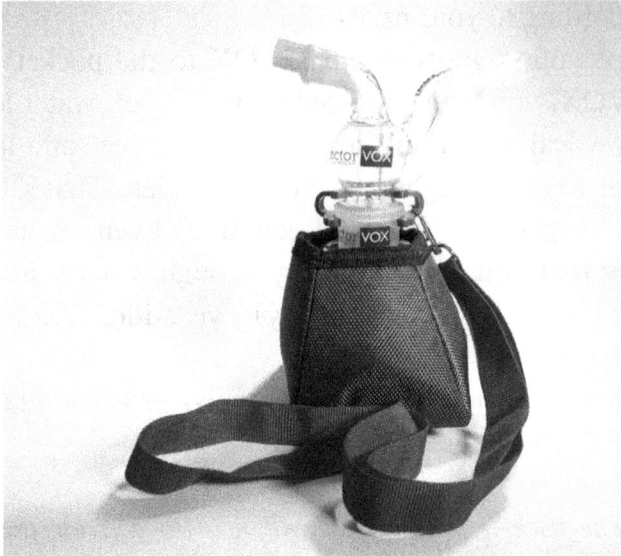

You can also add drops of liquid herbs or essential oils to the water, so that when you inhale, you breathe the herbs/oil down your trachea, onto your cords, and into your lungs. I've personally used colloidal silver, Thieves oil, and Synergy Oil (TMRG Solutions).

MaskVOX Setup

Since you already have a basic understanding of the pocketVOX from previous chapters, now it's time to learn how to attach the maskVOX to your pocketVOX. You can attach the maskVOX to the pocketVOX with two clicks. It is slightly different when using with the DoctorVOX.

I personally place one finger inside the mask against the hole and hold the long tube of the pocketVOX in the other hand, close to the tip opening. I then push the pocketVOX tip into the maskVOX tip until I hear two clicks and feel the pocketVOX tip press against my finger on the inside of the mask. See the video for further instruction.

MaskVOX Setup

Once it's set up, try singing through it. You can strap the maskVOX to your head or hold it against your mouth. I don't strap it to my head (as noted in the video) so that I can pull it away and take a mouth breath if I like. But please note that there is nothing wrong with nasal breathing. Also, my head is oddly shaped, haha, so it doesn't sit right with the strap. So I push and hold the maskVOX against my face.

What I've noticed when using the maskVOX:

- It will feel like a vacuum on your face when it's working properly.

- It makes your voice sound like it is far away, in a box, which is great for sound dampening when you need to lower the volume.

- You must learn to breathe in through the nose so you don't suck up water into the mask itself. If you mouth inhale, you will pull water up the pocketVOX tube.

- The voice feels and sounds more stable when the water level is lower.

- Like using the pocketVOX, using the maskVOX will make your throat feel like it is being massaged.

- The voice can become warbly and crack when the water level is too high.

In fact, you'll learn that you'll most likely need to decrease the water level once you've attached the maskVOX. This is because of the additional air mass that now exists within the interior of the maskVOX. This additional mass will add more "vocal weight" and can make it a little more difficult to bubble water than when using the pocketVOX alone. Adjust the water level as needed.

Breathing Exercises

When performing breathing exercises from my book *The Ultimate Breathing Workout* or the *Beyond the Ultimate Breathing Workout* video, you can use the maskVOX with the Lax Vox tube attached (without water) to create breathing resistance. Think of it as using weights for the lungs.

MaskVOX Breathing Exercises

Noise Reduction
In a pinch, you can also use the maskVOX by itself to reduce decibel levels when in an environment where you wish not to be heard. For example, if you're in a small bathroom behind the stage in a venue where you're getting ready to perform and you just want to sing over a few parts, you could use the maskVOX by itself to reduce the volume. I instantly discovered this benefit upon my first trial. It even replaced another device I've used called the BeltBox, because it's easier to pack and take with me on the road (and I take it with me regardless.)

MaskVOX Noise Reduction

Practicing on the Road
It can be difficult to drive and use a pocketVOX in a bottle of water. Hey, I still do it, but that means only one hand on the wheel, so I cannot in good conscience suggest you do the same. Since we want everyone to drive safely with both hands on the wheel, you could use the Lax Vox tube by itself without water for your vocal exercises or wear the maskVOX by itself to sing in the car (no Lax Vox tube attached unless desired).

Yes, I promise that you WILL get some funny looks, but if your goal is to build the best voice possible, take advantage of your driving time.

Now that I've offered some tips on how to use each device by itself, let's move to the next chapter, where I'll cover my special Isolation workout routine developed specifically for DoctorVOX Vocal Strength Training kit users.

CHAPTER SIX

— *Vocal Weightlifting Routines* —

As most of my students know, I consider myself more of a vocal strength trainer than a vocal coach. My specialty is keeping singers on the stage and in the studio by building vocal muscle. For years, students have come to me to develop their voices through my "vocal strength training" methods in order to increase vocal range, power, projection, and stage/studio stamina in order to perform night after night and sing take after take in the vocal booth.

The DoctorVOX Vocal Strength Training kit is the next logical step in vocal strength training, which is why I coined the term, "vocal weightlifting" several years ago when I started using DoctorVOX tools.

When using DoctorVOX devices you ARE lifting weight with your voice! Every ounce of water that you "push with your voice" equals a certain amount of "weight" in back pressure. So, are you ready to lift some weight with your voice to develop those vocal muscles?

I knew you were ready!

Following are two separate vocal weightlifting routines you can use with the DoctorVOX Vocal Strength Training kit to improve your vocal flexibility, get over vocal hurdles, smooth out vocal breaks, and increase your range, stamina, and power:

Vocal Weightlifting Routine #1:

Alternating Isolation Exercises

The first routine is your basic three-exercise Isolation routine. The only difference is that each pitch is repeated twice; the first time with pocketVOX and/or maskVOX, and the second time without the pocketVOX and/or maskVOX.

This routine is self-explanatory, but I will provide a video and offer one example of how to use each tool.

Falsetto Slides

In this example, I will perform the basic Falsetto Slide with the pocketVOX alone. Remember, there are four basic versions of each Isolation exercise, as explained in *Raise Your Voice*. We delve deeper into each exercise in Vendera Vocal Academy, so if you wish to follow along with your Weekly Academy Workouts, you can incorporate these tools by using your chosen combination of these devices with your Weekly Workouts. When following along with VVA workout videos, you do NOT have to repeat each pitch twice. Simply use the pocketVOX and/or maskVOX as you vocalize each pitch on each exercise in the workout video.

Falsetto Slide Example

Transcending Tones

I will perform the basic Transcending Tone exercise using only a Lax Vox tube. As I transcend from falsetto to full voice, I will slowly raise my Lax Vox tube from the bottom of the water bottle to the top (but keeping the bottom of the tube in water). This decreases the volume of water pressure, which aids in better glottal closure. Dr. Denizoglu says that using a tube in this manner with this exercise *increases control on phonation, which is good for singers.* Remember, this tube is optional, but can be purchased at DoctorVOX.US.

Transcending Tone Example

Sirens

I will perform a basic full voice Siren sliding up using a maskVOX attached to a pocketVOX. Remember to stay in a loud, full, resonant tone on this exercise. Though similar, the Siren is NOT the Corridor exercise, because we are going to maintain a full voice tone, not a blend (or mixed voice). You can, however, apply the Corridor visual on ANY exercise. Using these tools on Sirens might make you feel like you're not producing as loud and as powerful a tone as needed, but if the water is bubbling and you are sure you're in full voice, then I promise you that you're loud and powerful enough.

Siren Example

Other Vendera-Related Exercises

You can also use these tools with any exercise I teach, including E-screams, Grit Swells, Ultimate Isolation exercises, Vocal Power scales, and Sabine call-out exercises. Bottom line, back pressure will enhance the effectiveness and ease of any given vocal exercise.

Vocal Weight Lifting Routine #2:
Four-Week Vocal Power Routine

Yeah, the name of this routine is a nod to my vocal coach, Jim Gillette. Those of you using my books and products such as *The Four-Week Vocal Break Eraser* program know that I am a huge lover of four-week or 28-day programs. I've always been told that it takes 28 days to break a bad habit and/or establish a new good habit. Hey, sometimes I even shoot for five weeks. ;)

So, why should the Vendera Vox Trainer routine be any different? Hahaha, it's not! The following routine is a simple approach for building vocal power over four weekly workout phases that gradually add more time and "weight" to your vocal workout routine each week.

Simply follow the time guidelines for each week. You can use a stopwatch or set alarms on your smartphone. For those of you using my app, Tuned XD, you can set the Tabata timer to walk all the way through each time without having to reset the clock. Here's the breakdown:

PHASE ONE
Water Level– Find your best water level
The Falsetto Slide– 2 minutes
The Transcending Tone– 2 minutes
The Siren– 2 minutes
The Singing Routine– 15 minutes
Total Time = 21 minutes

PHASE TWO
Water Level– Increase water level by one mark
The Falsetto Slide– 3 minutes
The Transcending Tone– 3 minutes
The Siren– 3 minutes
The Singing Routine– 30 minutes
Total Time = 39 minutes

PHASE THREE
Water Level– Increase water level by one mark
The Falsetto Slide– 4 minutes
The Transcending Tone– 4 minutes
The Siren– 4 minutes
The Singing Routine– 45 minutes
Total Time = 57 minutes

PHASE FOUR
Water Level– Increase water level by one mark
The Falsetto Slide– 5 minutes
The Transcending Tone– 5 minutes
The Siren– 5 minutes
The Singing Routine– 60 minutes
Total Time= 75 minutes

WOW, you jumped from only 21 minutes of exercises and singing ALL the way up to 75 minutes in only four weeks!!! Hey, that's nothing! You probably sing more than 75 minutes per day!

Notice that I didn't include your *Voice RX Warmup*. That warmup is a given, and I'm assuming you woke up, performed your warmup routine, started your day, and worked out your voice at a different time. I do understand that some of you might wipe out your entire warmup and workout routine together in the morning, so just figure in another 15 minutes per session to include your warmup.

As for the actual "workout routine," I strongly suggest that you perform the workout session in the exact order presented. Make sure to do the exercises in the exact order and then move right into singing.

Better yet, use *V24* from SingBetterFast.com for the best Isolation routine. Don't forget to use your pocketVOX!

> **Bonus** – If you're familiar with *Jim Gillette's Vocal Power* program (which also has four phases), you can slip in Jim's scales right before your singing routine; speaking of which, back to singing …

For your daily singing sessions, choose the songs you love to sing, add them to a playlist, and check the time to make sure it surpasses the required time for singing. The time for the songs will never come out to be exactly what each week requires, so just make sure that last song goes past the required time. If you sing an extra two to three minutes, consider it a bonus!

Please note that it is also okay if you wish to start slower and attack singing like I have in my therapy sessions, by adding one song per week (or every two weeks like I am doing) for an allotted number of weeks (12–20 weeks should be sufficient). Once you've hit Week Four, you'd simply maintain your current Isolation times and add one more song per week as the weeks progress.

Regardless of your game plan, if you follow the core of the routine for the next four weeks, I guarantee you'll see amazing results!

That is it!
I'm done!!
I'm out of here!!!

Remember, this book is more of a "bonus manual" to accompany the DoctorVOX Vocal Strength Training kit, not a full-blown book, which is why I kept it small. If you want more detailed information on my methods, go to venderapublishing.com for *Raise Your Voice, Mind Over Music,* and all other books; visit VenderaVocalAcademy.com to join my online school; go to JaimeVendera.com for booking voice lessons, and to join my mailing list; and visit SingBetterFast.com for my podcast.

Don't forget to visit DoctorVOX.US to purchase additional DoctorVOX Vocal Strength Training kits and Superior Vocal Health products. While there, I suggest that you order extra pocketVOX devices because I guarantee you'll lose one on the road. I've done it and so have others, so I always carry triple supplies. :)

See you in my next book,

—Jaime Vendera

CHAPTER SEVEN

— Q&A —

Before I let you go, I'll finish this book with a little Q&A featuring some short and sweet answers to questions I've been asked concerning how to use the DoctorVOX Vocal Strength Training kit with my other products and methods.

Can I overuse the DoctorVOX Vocal Strength Training kit?

No. If you follow the guidelines in this booklet, and set your water level correctly, the back pressure massage effect prevents you from wearing out your voice.

If I use the DoctorVOX Vocal Strength Training kit all day long, will it hurt my voice?

Only when used incorrectly. See above answer.

I have vocal nodules, will the DoctorVOX Vocal Strength Training kit heal them?

In conjunction with a DVT program, Dr. Denizoglu has been very successful in reversing and eliminating vocal nodules and other vocal issues. Please consult Dr. Denizoglu in conjunction with your own ENT.

How long should I use the DoctorVOX Vocal Strength Training kit to warm up before a gig?

As long as needed. Some singers do a 15-minute warmup, while others use it throughout the day up until minutes before a performance.

Can I skip the four-week vocal weight lifting plan and use the DoctorVOX Vocal Strength Training kit with your V24 program?

Yes. As long as you follow the guidelines in this booklet, you can use your DoctorVOX Vocal Strength Training kit with any vocal workout.

Can I use the DoctorVOX Vocal Strength Training kit with a regular scale routine, such as Jim Gillette's Vocal Power exercises?

Yes. You'll recall that I slipped Jim's scales into Vocal Weightlifting Routine #2.

Can I use the DoctorVOX Vocal Strength Training kit with my Weekly Workouts from Vendera Vocal Academy?

Absolutely!

Can I use the DoctorVOX Vocal Strength Training kit with the Four Week Vocal Break Eraser program?

Yes.

Can the DoctorVOX Vocal Strength Training kit help me learn to scream or sing with grit?

Yes, but it will take some time getting used to the new sensations, especially when using the maskVOX. You will find that exercises like grit swells and exercises from the *Extreme Scream* series become easier when using a maskVOX.

I notice that I have a lot of vibrato when I sustain notes while using the pocketVOX/maskVOX? What's going on?

All is fine. Everything is in balance when you hear natural pitch vibrato occur.

I cannot tell if the water is bubbling the entire time. What do I do?

If you have a DoctorVOX device or a clear bottle for your pocketVOX, simply watch yourself in a mirror to see the water bubble. If you have a bottleVOX, you will feel the bubbling vibrations as you hd the bottle in the center at the hourglass indenture. You can also place your pinky on the bottom of the bottleVOX. This is a trick that I learned from my student, Carl Wyatt. He even says that he feels even more vibration when his pinky is pressed against the crease line on the bottom of the bottle.

I want to perform Shiatsu of the voice on myself. Is that okay?

I feel the same way but, no, you cannot perform Shiatsu of the voice on yourself. This is a very delicate procedure, both within the throat on the pharyngeal wall and on various pressure points on the neck and around the larynx. Incorrectly performing shiatsu of the voice can cause momentary blackout. Please contact Dr. Denizoglu to schedule an appointment or to inquire about other ENTs that might be offering Shiatsu of the voice treatments.

How do I clean my DoctorVOX tools?

Refer to the cleaning and maintenance section in this book, written by Claude LaRoche.

How long do DoctorVOX tools last?

Generally, they can last for months to years if cleaned and maintained properly. If you notice that the rubber begins to look dull and the surface becomes powdery, it is time to replace your pocketVOX or maskVOX or the tuner tips that come with the DoctorVOX device.

ABOUT THE AUTHORS

JAIME VENDERA is the author of dozens of books, audio programs, and video training programs, including *Raise Your Voice, Unleash Your Creative Mindset, SingFit, The Ultimate Breathing Workout, Mind Over Music,* The *Extreme Scream* audio series, The *Beyond the Voice* video series, and the vocal training app for iOS, *TUNED XD.*

He owns and operates Vendera Publishing and 711 Press.

Jaime is also the first documented singer on film to shatter a glass by the power of his voice alone, as seen on over 60 television shows worldwide, including, MythBusters, Dr. Oz, The Truth (UpRoxx), and Superhuman Showdown.

He is also a highly sought-after vocal coach, having an

uncanny ability to help singers build and release more range, power, and stamina than ever thought possible. Some of his clients have included singers from the bands Dream Theater, Starset, Skyharbor, Palisades, Hinder, Thriving Ivory, I Prevail, and many more touring and recording stars. He also teaches these same methods he developed for more vocal range, power, projection, and stamina through his online school, Vendera Vocal Academy. He lives with his wife, Diane, in Ohio.

Jaime can be contacted at:
JaimeVendera.com.
DoctorVOX.US
VenderaPublishing.com
VenderaVocalAcademy.com

Follow Jaime Vendera:
Twitter: https://twitter.com/jaimevendera
Instagram: instagram.com/jaimevendera/
Facebook: facebook.com/thejaimevendera
YouTube: youtube.com/user/venderaj
Soundcloud: soundcloud.com/vssounds

MD, Laryngology
MSc, Audiology and Speech Pathology
PhD (candidate) Biophysics

DR. ILTER DENIZOGLU is the director of the Clinical Vocology Department in MedicalPark Izmir Hospital, in Izmir, Turkey. His medical practice is focused primarily on phonosurgery, voice therapy, and singing voice therapy as well. He is also working as a university lecturer of pedagogical vocology in three different university's singing schools, including Dokuz Eylul University, Ege University, and Yasar University.

He has designed a set of surgical instruments for phonosurgery and also new devices for voice therapy and vocal training, including the Laryngoaltimeter, Vocal Posturometer and NIPA. His new vocal therapy and vocal training devices for singers, the DoctorVOX device, pocketVOX, and maskVOX are tools for Doctor Vox Voice (DVT) Therapy Technique, which he has been working on for over fifteen years.

He is an amateur singer and interested in music in almost every field, including singing voice therapy, singing pedagogy, music history, musical acoustics.

His ongoing studies for Biophysics and Audiology and Speech Pathology are part of his enthusiasm about completing the whole picture of human voice in the name of basic, clinical, and pedagogical vocology.

He can be contacted through doctorvox.com.

www.ingramcontent.com/pod-product-compliance
Lightning Source LLC
Chambersburg PA
CBHW060421090426
42734CB00011B/2402